South Australia

"South Australia" is published by the South Australian Government for distribution throughout the world to organisations and individuals interested in the progress and development of the State of South Australia.

COVER by Peter Richards.

Dawn of a new age in the South Australian Outback. Early morning sun breaks through the clouds at Olympic Dam—site of the vast riches of the already legendary Roxby Downs mineral resource development in South Australia's harsh outback region. Estimates of the true value of Roxby Downs' lode of copper, gold, uranium, rare earths and other deposits is being constantly revised upwards as new resources are detected and assessed. The deposit is already being called the "Zambia copper belt" of the future and "one of the richest mineral deposits anywhere on earth".

Major photographic contributions from Peter Richards and Milton Wordley.

Coordination and original design by State Promotion Unit Office of State Development.

Printed at Griffin Press Limited, Netley, South Australia.

National Library of Australia's Cataloguing-in-Publication data Department of the Premier and Cabinet, South Australia.
"South Australia"
SBN 0 7243 3457 3

MESSAGE FROM THE PREMIER

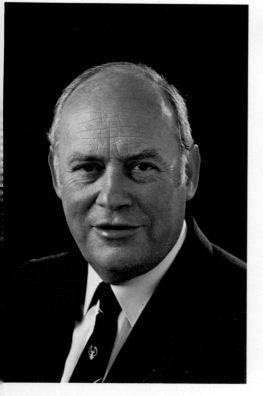

South Australia is on the verge of a new and exciting era in its development.

It is the State emerging as Australia's new frontier.

This book is designed to provide a brief picture of South Australia's investment future and at the same time illustrate the characteristics which make it a unique region in which to live and work.

In 1986 South Australia will celebrate its 150th Anniversary, yet only now is the full potential of the State's mineral wealth being recognised. South Australia is the only State which was not originally established as a penal colony. The first pioneers who settled in 1836 came of their own free choice to start a new life in a harsh and hostile environment.

This tradition of fierce independence, established by the early German and Cornish pioneers, has become a characteristic of South Australia and its people.

Author Douglas Pike described South Australia as "a paradise of dissent" and this is reflected in the leadership shown by this State in areas such as women's voting.

From these beginnings, the State has developed as a truly multi-cultural society, a community which is the centre of Australia's artistic life.

The majority of South Australia's 1.3 million people live in the capital city Adelaide which, as this book endeavours to illustrate, provides an ideal living and working environment free of the problems of pollution and over-crowding which beset larger cities.

South Australia's attractive lifestyle is heightened by a snow-free mediterranean climate ideal for wine production and a wide variety of sporting and other recreational activities.

South Australia's wine, particularly from the Barossa Valley, is now winning world acclaim and penetrating markets in Asia and North America.

The State also produces vast quantities of wheat and barley and is one of Australia's major wool growing areas.

While South Australia was built on the foundations created by the rural industries, its future growth and prosperity now appear to rest with the vast mineral wealth which lies below the ground.

Although many deposits of natural gas, oil, coal and uranium are still the subject of study and assessment it is likely that by the end of this century South Australia will be the major supplier of energy to the world.

The Cooper Basin in the north of the State has enormous potential for further development. Other mining projects including the copper/gold/uranium deposit known as Roxby Downs have the potential to become world class mining projects.

The wealth beneath the ground is now the subject of intense study by overseas investors who are considering projects which will attract billions of dollars to the State.

South Australia has a large and important manufacturing base with its activity concentrated in steel production, in motor vehicle manufacturing operation and in the white goods industry. More and more, these industries are diversifying and tailoring their operations to suit an ever-expanding export market, and are proving that quality South Australian made products can compete with the best in the the world. In many respects, South Australian-based companies have unique advantages over their interstate counterparts. Production costs, for example, are considerably lower than in the major eastern States of Victoria and New South Wales; our record of industrial disputes, in terms of man hours lost, is the lowest of any State; and industrial land in Adelaide is more than 50% cheaper than comparable land in either Sydney or Melbourne.

Another major factor in our favour is South Australia's central geographical position. We are at the hub of Australia's transport system, and efficient transport systems which serve the State move personnel and goods safely, rapidly and economically without compromising fuel conservation.

The South Australian Government firmly believes that by far the major part of Australia's development in the future will be based on the fortunes of South Australia, the Northern Territory and Western Australia. With our existing industrial base, South Australia is ideally placed to be at the forefront of that development. Incentives are available for those who wish to participate and share in the growth of South Australia. These include various taxation concessions, loans and cash grants to qualifying manufacturing and processing industries, Government infrastructure arrangements for large scale projects, and assistance with land, industrial premises and services. Special concessions for large-scale developments may also be given.

The South Australian Government will do whatever it can to assist new industries to establish, and established companies to expand. Naturally there are differences of philosophy between political parties but the Government's hopes and aspirations for South Australia's future prosperity are shared by all. Proposals for development projects would receive a full and open hearing from all South Australians.

Finally, South Australia has a government committed to the free enterprise ethic, one which recognises individual initiative, imagination, drive and effort.

We will be pleased to hear from anyone who would like to become part of South Australia's future. You may be sure of a warm welcome.

DAVID TONKIN
Premier

3

SOUTH AUSTRALIA
A STATE ON THE MOVE

Imagine a land mass almost eight times greater than England or one-and-a-half times the size of Texas. A region of strong contrasts and diversity in the natural environment and in the work and leisure of its people.

South Australia is Australia's fourth largest State—it occupies one eighth of the continent. Within its borders, the vast majority of the State's population live in cities and centres on the coast. One million people of the total population of 1.3 million live in the capital city of Adelaide.

While there are deserts that stretch for hundreds of kilometres, over one-half of South Australia is devoted to agriculture. Agriculture provided prosperity for South Australia in the beginnings of the colony.

The discovery of copper also contributed to the economic growth of the State. Now South Australia enters a new era of economic prosperity.

South Australia is the nation's last mineral resources frontier. In the last five years discoveries of oil, natural gas, copper, gold, uranium and coal have dramatically changed the minerals future for South Australia.

Apart from the underground wealth, South Australia, and Adelaide in particular, offer a wealth of cultural activity.

The City of Adelaide is "possibly the last well-planned, well-governed and moderately contented metropolis on earth" according to "The New Yorker" magazine. Settled by free men, Adelaide rests on a narrow coastal plain, between St. Vincent Gulf and the lush Mt. Lofty Ranges.

Adelaide offers a comfortable lifestyle with the advantages of big city living. It has more restaurants per head of population than any other Australian city.

The Adelaide Festival of Arts, held every two years, is internationally acclaimed. Performers and creative artists of Australian and international repute gather for the Festival, its principal venue being the Festival Centre, one of the most effective arts complexes in the world.

Sophistication in South Australia extends also to its industry. The State is fast becoming the centre for high technology industry in Australia.

With stable industry and government, a diversity of recreational and leisure opportunities, and its immense mineral resources, South Australia offers and will continue to offer a quality of life not easily surpassed.

A State of Contrasts

South Australia is about 1200 kilometres from east to west, and 1300 kilometres from north to south at its deepest point.

Within the 984,377 square kms of South Australia lies an immense variety of landscapes. It is a land of low relief, the inland area being largely covered by vast plains or sand and gibber (stone) deserts. Over 80 per cent of the State is less than 300 metres above sea level.

The Mount Lofty-Flinders Ranges system is the main mountainous feature, yet at its highest point it does not exceed 1166 metres.

On the other hand, the pattern of communication and development has been greatly influenced by the coastline, a coastline with long stretches of sandy beaches, and with rugged cliffs towering 120 metres.

The effect of the vast ocean to the south is a more temperate climate than would be suggested by the State's latitude, south of the 26th parallel. While summers are hot and dry with mild nights, winters are cool and wet. Coastal areas are exposed to westerly rainbearing air streams with most rainfall occurring from May to August. Snow is rare in South Australia.

High rainfall in the south-east of the State produces lush pastures for agriculture. South Australia is abundant with diverse and fascinating flora and fauna. A number of National Parks have been established to preserve examples of indigenous fauna, alongside agricultural and pastoral activities.

A Brief History

Settlement

Dutch, French and British explorers had sailed the coasts of South Australia before Matthew Flinders and Joseph Banks joined forces to circumnavigate the continent of Australia and chart the coast in detail. During the period of these voyages, sealers and runaway convicts were visiting Kangaroo Island, where from 1804 onwards, settlements were founded. Pressure of population in England, along with assurances that South Australia offered land fit for agriculture, led to decisions about it being a suitable place for a colony.

Colonel William Light sailed from England in May 1836 and, after some

Fireworks over the Adelaide Festival Centre during the Festival of Arts.

preliminary exploration of alternative sites, chose one on the banks of the River Torrens as the surveying area for the city of Adelaide. By the end of the following year, Light had completed the survey of Adelaide and designed a plan for the city. It was Light's vision which made possible the pleasant, efficient city that Adelaide is today.

The South Australian Colonisation Act was assented to in August 1834, the establishment and financing of government to be subsidised by loans raised by the Board of Commissioners, which controlled land sales and immigration.

The early years of the colony were not smooth but by 1844 the colony was producing wheat in excess of its needs and became self-supporting in 1845. Moreover, prosperity was on the doorstep; copper had been found at Kapunda in 1843 and a major find was made at Burra in 1845.

Heavy immigration followed these discoveries and continued until the Victorian gold rush. Copper soon became the principal export, with wool providing a complementary cargo.

The discovery of gold in Victoria in 1851 had a two-fold influence on the development of South Australia. In the first place it drained off a large proportion of the skilled artisans and forced the closing of the copper mines, and secondly it gave great impetus to agriculture when the price of wheat rose sharply. At the same time, political changes were taking place and in 1856 South Australia attained self-government. *The Constitution Act of 1855-56* provided for responsible government for South Australia at the hands of a Governor acting on behalf of the Monarch and upon advice from Her Ministers.

Exploration

Only a small part of the area proclaimed as South Australia was to prove economically viable. Extensive exploration, with its accompanying hardships, continued into the 1870s. Captain Charles Sturt, whose journey down the Murray in 1834 had helped to stimulate the colonisation of South Australia, was again to contribute to South Australian exploration. In search of an inland sea his expedition turned back 700 kilometres from the Gulf of Carpentaria. Other explorers who played their part in the discovery of South Australia's regions included Edward John Eyre, Colonel Frome, John McDouall Stuart and William Ernest Giles.

Government

South Australia is one of the six Australian States which at Federation in 1901 ceded many of their powers to the Commonwealth of Australia. In addition, powers on localised regional matters have been delegated to local governing bodies. As a result, the people of South Australia are subject to three tiers of government—Federal, State and Local. Both the Commonwealth and South Australian Parliaments are bicameral: in

each, the leader of the Government (the Prime Minister of the Commonwealth, and the Premier of the State) is seated in the Lower House and in each the Upper House has restricted powers concerning money Bills.

Ministers are chosen from elected Members of Parliament and are jointly responsible to the Parliament. Members of both Houses of Parliament are elected by secret ballot in a preferential system of voting. There is full adult franchise at the age of eighteen. South Australia takes pride in having been the first of the Australian States to extend the franchise to women.

The Legislative Council consists of 22 members elected for a term of six years, while the Lower House, the House of Assembly, has 47 electoral districts. Elections are to be held within three years.

Most members of both Commonwealth and State Parliaments are elected by the voters from candidates pre-selected and endorsed by major political parties. The South Australian Cabinet, while having no constitutional basis or power, is the central decision-making body of government. Cabinet decisions are implemented by appropriate elements within the structure of government and ratified by Executive Council, that is, the Governor of South Australia in Council with Ministers.

Cabinet and Executive Council are serviced by the Department of the Premier and Cabinet.

The People

Most South Australians are Australian-born and raised, and English speaking.

Although most South Australians have their origins in Britain, Ireland and other Commonwealth countries, significant contributions have been made by German, Italian, Greek and many other ethnic peoples to what is now a truly multi-cultural society.

There is a national policy on assisted migration from all countries. Assisted passages are now only given to skilled tradesmen and refugees. Indo-Chinese refugees now comprise about one-quarter of Australia's total immigration programme. South Australia has provided resettlement for a proportionate number of these refugees. South Australia's population is over 1.3 million with the vast majority living in Adelaide. Regional centres including Mount Gambier, Whyalla, Port Pirie, Port Augusta and Port Lincoln account for much of the remainder, leaving the rest of South Australia very sparsely populated.

The Potential

Until recently, South Australia, the nation's least minerally developed State, was known primarily as a high grade iron ore producer, as well as a leading opal producer.

Most of the world's precious opal is produced at Coober Pedy, Andamooka and Mintabie. Iron ore is mined in the

Middleback Ranges, west of Whyalla. Reserves of natural gas, now being piped to cities south and east, have altered the State's mineral profile, along with the development of liquid hydrocarbons. The largest resource development project ever undertaken in South Australia is in hand following ratification by the State Parliament of an Indenture Agreement which provides for the recovery, processing and marketing of crude oil and condensate from the Cooper Basin. In addition, feasibility studies are being undertaken with a view to the establishment of a petrochemical plant based on ethane from the Cooper Basin. Oil flows have been tapped in the State's far north, with a recently drilled well testing at a rate of 3600 barrels per day. This is the largest flow rate from a single oil reservoir onshore in Australia. Significant new discoveries of oil and gas continue to be made in hitherto untapped reservoirs.

Huge deposits of copper-uranium mineralisation exist at Roxby Downs Station in the north of the State—thought to be one of the world's largest, single, new concentrations of minerals to be discovered in fifty years—and extensive feasibility studies are underway.

Apart from the exciting future for South Australia in resource development, industrial development continues at a steady rate. The high technology sector of manufacturing industry is seen as a major growth area for South Australia. A most attractive lifestyle coupled with a stable democracy and the economic development underway means that South Australia is a State with a promising future.

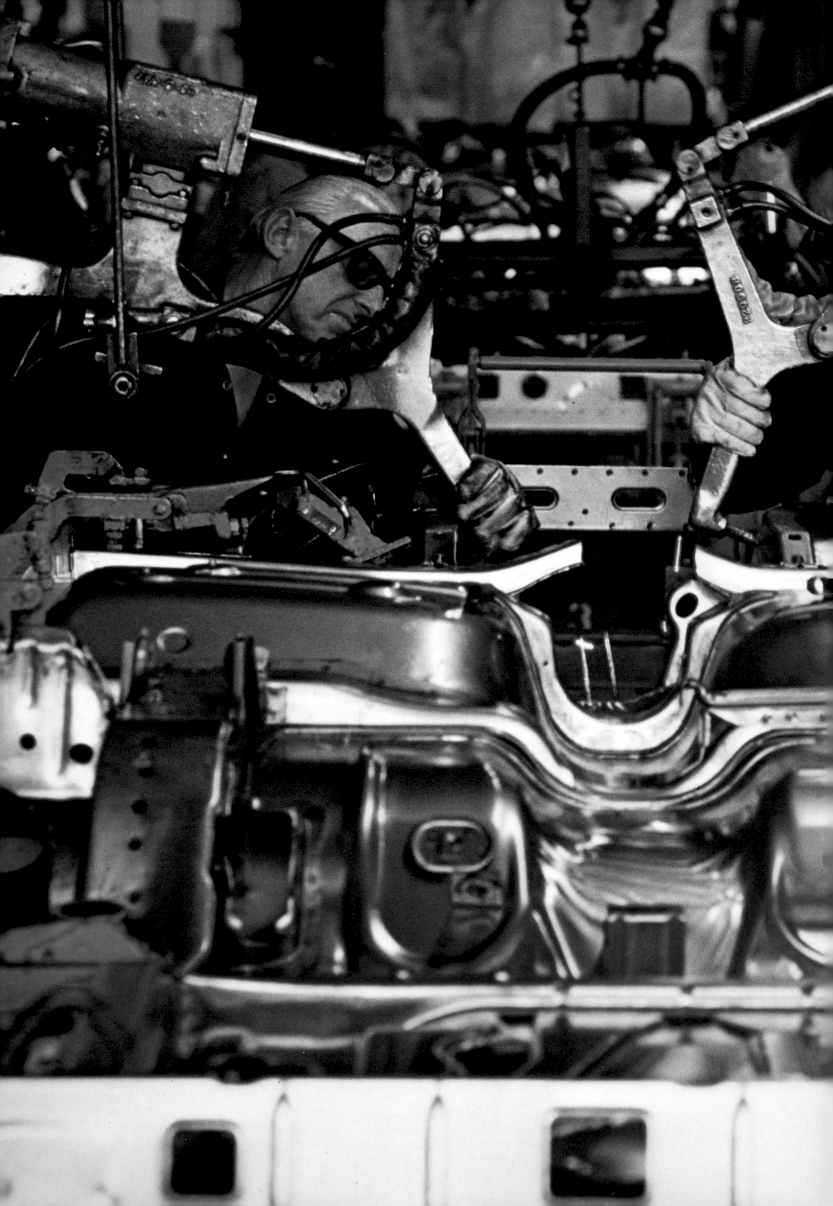

Part of a robot assembly mechanism used for motor car production.

INDUSTRY: PLANNING IN ACTION

Over the last three decades the economy of South Australia has been transformed from one based essentially on primary production to one chiefly dependent on the manufacturing and tertiary sectors.

Manufacturing activity in South Australia is diverse. Production of motor vehicles, domestic appliances, other forms of machinery and equipment, fabricated metal products and base metal products forms the industrial base. Production in textiles, clothing, footwear, wood and wood products, chemicals and plastics industries is significant.

High technology industries are also strongly represented in South Australia, with further strong growth expected in the communications field.

South Australia has shared, with the rest of Australia, in an economic growth period in which billions of dollars have been invested in this country, mainly from the United States of America, Great Britain, Japan and West Germany. This has given impetus to the nation's growth and its development as a logical supply base for South East Asia and the Pacific Basin.

The outlook in the State is positive, supported by the South Australian Government which places high priority on the economic growth and industrial development of the State.

The Government supports private enterprise by providing infrastructure and developing skills in the workforce.

The attractions to the investor are many. The State has a well-established industrial base, a central geographic location in relation to Australian markets, a highly skilled work force with a creditable labour relations record, and extensive and diverse mineral resources.

In addition, there is low-priced, well-serviced and conveniently located industrial land. General building costs compare favourably with other States while a lack of high density living, traffic congestion and other urban problems make South Australia an attractive alternative.

Industrial Success

There are many national and international companies that have invested in South Australia with good results, not to mention the many South Australians who have developed their own manufacturing companies with outstanding success.

Adelaide

The most important of the State's manufacturing interests is the motor vehicle industry. The international corporations, General Motors and Mitsubishi, have bases in Adelaide, supported by manufacturers of automobile components.

South Australia has a history of involvement with the motor car industry. In 1923, H. J. Holden began making motor bodies for General Motors. By 1931 his company was supplying all the bodies needed by General Motors for its Australian market. In that year General Motors (Aust.) Pty. Ltd. acquired his business and formed General Motors-Holden's Ltd.

Today, the plant at the original Woodville site covers an area of 186,000 square metres and its sister plant at Elizabeth occupies a similar area. These sites contain much of the in-house production of General Motors-Holden's Ltd., including body stamping and sheet metal operations, and some vehicle assembly.

Chrysler Australia Limited established its South Australian operation through the acquisition of a local motor body building firm, T. J. Richards and Sons, originally coach builders, who had begun making Dodge bodies in 1922. In 1947 Chrysler Dodge Distributors (Australia) Pty. Ltd. absorbed this firm, and was itself taken over in 1951 by the Chrysler Corporation, to form Chrysler Australia Limited. Ownership was transferred to Mitsubishi in 1980. Mitsubishi's main plants in Adelaide are at Tonsley Park and Lonsdale. Body sheet metal and assembly functions are at the Tonsley Park plant, while engines come from the Lonsdale operation.

In 1981, Mitsubishi Australia again produced Australia's largest selling 4-cylinder car, a position it has held for four years.

For many years, South Australia has been one of the nation's main producers of large household appliances such as refrigerators, washing machines and cookers. Other important production industries are air conditioning, water heating systems and other electrical and electronic machinery and components. Two local companies have influenced this development.

Simpson Ltd., now one of Australia's largest manufacturers of home appliances, originated in 1853 when Alfred Simpson set up shop in Adelaide as a tinsmith. The company's production now includes washing machines, cookers and other kitchen appliances, irrigation equipment, electric motors, bathroom fittings and tumble dryers.

Simpson has recently spent $6.5 million in establishing the most modern dishwasher manufacturing complex in Australia. This plant has been built at one of Adelaide's industrial estates, Regency Park.

Kelvinator Australia Limited pioneered the manufacture of domestic refrigerators in Australia and now produces a range of other electrical appliances including air conditioners and commercial cooling equipment.

Intensive involvement in the motor vehicle and domestic appliance industries has meant that South Australian tradesmen develop and retain special skills in such areas as the moulding and extrusion of plastics, toolmaking, presswork and aluminium casting.

Many smaller companies supply components for the motor vehicle and domestic appliance industries and have expanded their operations to produce for a wider range of industries.

In the field of electronics, Australia has generally been unable to compete at international levels of domestic electronic goods production. Nevertheless, South Australia has retained a sound nucleus of an electronics industry, particularly in the areas of professional electronics and communications.

The Commonwealth-operated defence research centres in this State (noted for expertise in sophisticated communication, telemetry, rocketry and guidance systems), have had significant influence in retaining electronics and communication skills by fostering the development of high technology support industries.

Fairey Australasia Pty. Ltd., in this same category of industries, manufactures precision tools, instruments, and specialised equipment for local and overseas markets. Practically all of the telemetry systems used in Jindivik target aircraft were manufactured by Fairey.

British Aerospace Australia, a member of the British Aerospace Group of Companies, moved to South Australia in 1959 and has since established itself as a designer/manufacturer of high technology electronic systems in defence and other related areas. Its special interests include thermal imaging, optical electronic tracking techniques and aircraft fatigue instrumentation.

EMI Electronics, a division of EMI (Australia) Limited, has been operating successfully since its establishment in South Australia in 1951. This is a high technology electronics company which undertakes engineering feasibility studies, design and development, manufacture, test and life-cycle support of complex computer-based systems and equipment for military and complementary non-military applications.

In 1959, EMI was selected to be involved in the development of the Ikara Shipborne Anti-submarine Weapons System as a contractor to the Weapons Research Establishment at Salisbury,

Assembly line quality control at Raytheons Ltd.

South Australia. This system is now being replaced by newer and more sophisticated programmes which cover a widening spectrum of electronic technology.

Sola International, which is now part of the Pilkington Group, is a local company which has made impressive progress since its establishment less than 20 years ago. From a small start in one room, the company now employs a large staff to make lenses and scientific optical instruments. The first American astronauts on the moon wore Sola CR39 sunglasses.

Raytheon International Data Systems, one of the leaders in office technology in Australia, has committed $5 million to establish and develop its new factory in Hendon, S.A.

Raytheon is the only company manufacturing word processing equipment and data processing screens in this State.

The chemical and plastics industries are expected to play a more important role in South Australia's future industrial development. Liquid hydrocarbons from the Cooper Basin in the north of the State are expected to provide the feedstock for a substantial petro-chemical industry, with prospects for "down-stream" industries.

This development will be a valuable addition to the State's existing industrial production which includes the operations of I.C.I. (Australia) Ltd., Petroleum Refineries (Australia) Ltd., and Adelaide and Wallaroo Fertilizers Ltd. Soda ash, caustic soda and calcium chloride as well as other minerals, are produced by I.C.I. at its Osborne plant and the Company has extensive salt fields north of Adelaide. Petroleum Refineries (Australia) Ltd. operates an oil refinery complex south of Adelaide at Port Stanvac. Adelaide and Wallaroo Fertilizers Ltd., specialises in the

Computerised lathe at John Shearer and Co.

production of chemical fertilisers, trace elements, acids and related products.

The plastics industry has developed rapidly, partly to meet the needs of the motor vehicle and domestic appliance industries. It now has special capabilities in plastic extrusion and injection moulding to produce small to relatively large components.

Companies with manufacturing facilities in Adelaide are marketing their products locally, nationally and internationally.

Those with success in exporting include:
John Shearer Ltd., an agricultural equipment manufacturer exporting to the Middle East;
Actil Ltd. exporting bed linen to South East Asia;
Atco Industries Ltd. is supplying accommodation facilities for overseas projects;
Australian Bacon Ltd. has had successful sales of meat, smallgoods and frozen foods overseas.

Regional Centres

The State's manufacturing industry is located predominantly in or near Adelaide.

However, regional centres at Whyalla, Port Pirie, Port Augusta and Mount Gambier are well-established with an infrastructure sophisticated enough to support further industrial development. In these and other provincial cities the presence of mineral and other resources has stimulated the growth of basic metal, timber, related industries and support services.

Whyalla

Industrial development at Whyalla on the north-west coast of Spencer Gulf has centred around the steel making complex operated by the Broken Hill Proprietary Company Ltd., which takes its iron ore supplies from the substantial deposits in the Middleback Ranges.

The amazing dishwasher production line
at Simpsons.

Whyalla steelworks.

Body assembly work at General Motors Holden.

Safety belt release mechanisms at Rainsfords.

The BHP operations at Whyalla include an integrated iron and steel works of world scale. As well as BHP, Whyalla supports a variety of other industries with emphasis in heavy engineering.

One of the most important economic developments in South Australia is located at Stony Point, 20 kilometres north of Whyalla.

The construction of a fractionation plant and associated facilities to process the Cooper Basin liquid hydrocarbons is providing major contract work for Whyalla companies and employment opportunities.

Port Pirie
On the eastern shores of Spencer Gulf, Port Pirie is the closest port to the rich lead-zinc mines of Broken Hill (New South Wales).

Ore concentrates from these mines are railed to Port Pirie to the Broken Hill Associated Smelters Pty. Limited, which is the largest lead smelting and refining plant in the world. The refinery also produces zinc, silver, gold, cadmium, copper matte, and antimonial lead alloys. There is a thriving fishing industry as well as service industries.

Port Augusta
Port Augusta, at the head of Spencer Gulf, is at the apex of the so-called Iron Triangle. It is also the junction for the north-south and east-west road and rail traffic across the continent. Australian National, the railways authority, has its maintenance headquarters there. The expansion of the railway operations, the standardisation of the east-west system and the new rail link to Alice Springs in the Northern Territory will ensure the future growth of the city as a transport centre.

A significant percentage of South Australia's electrical power is generated at Port Augusta's Thomas Playford Power

Station, using coal from the Leigh Creek deposit in the far north of the State and construction of a larger power station is underway.

The Iron Triangle Study
A high-level development team is conducting the Iron Triangle Study to investigate and identify the potential of this particular region.

Whyalla, Port Pirie and Port Augusta offer a region that has unique opportunities for resource-associated development.

Mount Gambier
Mount Gambier is located in the south-east of the State, mid-way on the Princes Highway between Adelaide and Melbourne. Mount Gambier has a range of established industries and the potential for significant growth. Extensive plantations of Pinus radiata have been the base for a timber industry in a State deficient in indigenous forests.

The government and a number of private firms run several large sawmills, particle board factories and pressure treatment plants producing timber mainly for construction purposes. The main private companies are Softwood Holdings Limited, Sapfor Timber Mills Limited and Mount Gambier Pine Industries Pty. Limited. In addition, two large paper mills near Millicent, Cellulose Australia Limited and Apcel Pty. Limited, manufacture cardboard and tissue paper. Market gardening, dairying and livestock production, which take advantage of the fertile soils of the region, form a basis for a variety of processing industries. Further natural resources supporting secondary industry are the Mount Gambier limestone deposits and a large reserve of naturally-occurring carbon dioxide. Fletcher Jones and Staff Pty. Ltd. is a firm which has recognised the advantages of Mount Gambier's decentralised location,

well-established service facilities, and stable female workforce. The company manufactures high quality clothing.

Other Areas
Other country centres, which investors may find attractively located, are Port Lincoln and the towns along the upper part of the River Murray; a region known as the Riverland.

Port Lincoln already has a substantial fish-processing industry based on tuna and other fishing in the Great Australian Bight. It is also the main outlet for the wheat of Eyre Peninsula.

The Riverland towns base their industry mainly on the processing of fruit grown in the area.

There are canneries, wineries and associated activities at Renmark, Barmera, Berri, Loxton and Waikerie.

Development in South Australia has been achieved without the problems which have beset many countries and cities. Effective planning has provided for industrial expansion away from residential areas, with less pollution problems. In the metropolitan area, the free-flow of traffic results in lower internal transport costs.

Transport for the Industry
The South Australian economy is well served by an expanding major port facility at the Port of Adelaide, by a versatile and efficient road transport system, rail services to all industrial centres and comprehensive inter and intrastate air services.

Excellent cargo handling facilities and adequate store accommodation at the Port of Adelaide ensure efficient and rapid turn around of shipping and cargo. Ports such as Port Pirie, Whyalla, Port Augusta, Ardrossan, Wallaroo and Port Lincoln are strategically located along the South Australian seaboard.

Major industries are provided with spur

lines to permit swift movement of products by rail. Container freighting and standardisation have brought about increased efficiency in the rail system. Sophisticated vehicles and modern organisational techniques make daily express services on a door-to-door basis possible for all kinds of freight cargos. The South Australian transport industry benefits from the fact that freight flow in this country is heavily weighted by traffic travelling east. This means attractive rates can be negotiated for freight being shipped from South Australia to eastern states' markets. Freight rates in South Australia are among the lowest in Australia.

A comprehensive picture of South Australia's transport system is in "ADELAIDE—THE CENTRE OF IT ALL".

Land and Services

Industrial Land

The government's policy is to ensure that the State can offer a plentiful supply of low-cost industrial land close to housing estates, shopping centres and port facilities.

In the metropolitan area and in selected regional centres, the South Australian Housing Trust (a State Government statutory Authority) has purchased large areas of land for development as industrial sites.

Industries with specific siting requirements such as proximity to harbour facilities or to the central business district have a choice of reasonably priced and well-situated sites. The State Department of Marine and Harbors has a substantial area of land located about 14 kilometres from the centre of Adelaide, adjacent to the Port of Adelaide. For industries that require land as close as possible to the main business area of Adelaide, there are still some parcels of privately owned or government land available at prices considerably lower than those of comparable sites in other Australian cities. Industries preferring decentralised locations have available to them a wide choice of sites in South Australian country towns, where low-cost industrial land is readily accessible.

Water

Water supply in South Australia is managed by the government's Engineering and Water Supply Department to allow for the needs of continuing growth. Eight major reservoirs in the Mount Lofty Ranges and two pipelines from the River Murray ensure adequate water for Adelaide's industrial and domestic requirements.

The Water Resources Branch of the Department can provide a large amount of relevant data for industry and business which require water. Adelaide is also the best served capital in the country with about 97 per cent of the metropolitan area connected to an efficient sewerage and sewerage treatment system.

Fuel pipelines at Port Stanvac.

Power

The availability and cost of energy must concern prospective investors. Proven resources show that South Australia has, in addition to significant natural gas and oil deposits, large reserves of coal sufficient to provide its energy requirements for many decades. Energy costs in South Australia are competitive with those prevailing in other parts of Australia, and are lower than in overseas oil-dependent nations.

The Electricity Trust of South Australia is continually extending its power generation capacity to meet industrial and domestic needs. Natural gas, piped from the Cooper Basin in the State's far north is distributed by the South Australian Gas Company to domestic and industrial users in the metropolitan area of Adelaide, to rural areas of the State and also to Sydney and Canberra.

Technology Park Adelaide

The South Australian Government has initiated a unique high technology/ science based industrial estate called Technology Park Adelaide. It has been conceived as Australia's first comprehensively planned centre for scientific research and development and high technology industry.

The aim of TPA will be achieved through site planning and development and the establishment of formal links with Adelaide's major tertiary education institutions.

TPA will be located adjacent to The Levels campus of the South Australian Institute of Technology, 10 kilometres north of Adelaide. It is envisaged that tenants will have ready access to the specialised equipment, research facilities and labour resources of the major tertiary educational institutions in South Australia. The Park will be attractively landscaped into three precincts separated by buffer zones.

Fuel storage tanks at Port Stanvac.

Precinct 1—Research and Development is for individuals or organisations undertaking projects ranging from original experimental work to development and testing for established enterprises. This area is adjacent to the SAIT campus to facilitate liaison between tenants and the Institute.
Precinct 2—High Technology/Science Based Industry will cater mainly for enterprises undertaking the manufacture or assembly of high technology products intended for firms appreciating the asset of a high quality environment and employing professional and skilled personnel.
Precinct 3—Mining/Energy Orientated Research and Development Organisations. This area will be allocated for research stations and associated laboratories and pilot plants.
Site development of Technology Park Adelaide is underway and it is expected the Park will be operational by the end of 1982.

Industrial Relations

The industrial relations record in South Australia is excellent. With 9 per cent of the nation's workforce, industrial disputes in the State have consistently represented less than 4 per cent of the Australian total. The South Australian Government is determined further to improve industrial relations to ensure the development of industry and security of employment. This policy can best be achieved by co-operation between employers and employees and it is the government's objective to provide the most effective framework to ensure meaningful conciliation and negotiation followed by fair arbitration.

In an age of rapidly changing technology, automation and international competition, the survival and growth of industry will depend upon technical and managerial skills.

Miners gear at Roxby Downs.

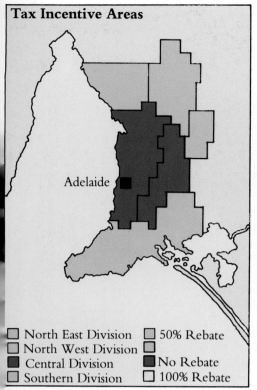

Tax Incentive Areas

Adelaide

- ☐ North East Division
- ☐ North West Division
- ■ Central Division
- ☐ Southern Division
- ☐ 50% Rebate
- ☐
- ■ No Rebate
- ☐ 100% Rebate

South Australian Investment Seminar in Tokyo 1982.

o meet these needs the South Australian Government is revising industrial and commercial training to provide a new, unified approach to vocational training in his State.

he State Government has also set up a Council on Technological Change which to study the effects such change will have on society and recommend ways of etting the maximum benefit from adopting new technology. The overnment is firmly committed to a policy of using high technology to keep outh Australian industry competitive. Over the past few years there has been a eady fall in the number of industrial accidents in the State. Through the Department of Industrial Affairs and mployment the government is onstantly monitoring and considering ways of improving industrial safety. he department employs an expert on isk Management to advise both the public and private sectors on ways of voiding accidents as well as reducing the fects of unavoidable traumas.

fety committees are regarded as useful nd are recommended within the ructure of employee participation hich is encouraged in South Australian dustry—and has been adopted ccessfully in enterprises ranging from age multi-national plants to small wner-managed businesses.

dustrialists need expect little difficulty securing a stable workforce of the propriate skills, in this State. They will nd that wage rates in South Australia are nerally lower than in the other major ates.

ne government is pledged to the full velopment of South Australia's dustrial potential and has created a wide nge of services designed to encourage ablishment of industry. South ustralian Government assistance to dustry is co-ordinated through the epartment of the Premier and Cabinet th the Department of Trade and dustry playing an active role in

commercial and industrial development. Because of its involvement in the motor vehicle, electronics and defence industries, South Australia has developed a highly skilled workforce.

Government Assistance
A comprehensive package of financial assistance measures is offered to new or expanding industries in South Australia. It includes:

Industrial Premises
Under this scheme the government can assist eligible applicants by providing low-cost industrial land. Design and construction of factory premises can be assisted. Land and premises are made available under an attractive lease/purchase arrangement which enables firms to buy during the lease term at a predetermined price that takes into account previous lease payments.

Establishment Payments
Cash grants are made to eligible firms which create additional employment opportunities in the State by establishing a new industry or expanding an existing operation.

Finance
Finance may be made available to firms during early stages of development, by way of loans, grants or equity participation. Also, government guarantees are given to facilitate borrowing through the banking systems.

State Tax Rebates
Firms manufacturing outside metropolitan Adelaide may qualify, on location criteria, for 50 to 100 per cent rebate of payroll and land tax. In addition, the government offers generous payroll tax incentives to encourage industries to employ workers under 20 years of age. Industries establishing in South Australia are assured of minimum interference but

full support and encouragement from the government. Through the Department of the Premier and Cabinet and the Department of Trade and Industry, firms can be assisted with a wide range of matters, especially where these involve dealings with Federal, State and Local Governments.

Overseas Investment
Although there are no legislative provisions requiring local participation in the capital or management of companies set up in Australia by overseas interests, the government encourages opportunities for Australian enterprises which offer equity in Australia.

Association may range from production by the Australian firm under licence or royalty agreements, to the setting-up of a new Australian company in which the provision of both capital and management is shared.

Exchange control is administered in accordance with the policy of encouraging overseas investment in Australia. While all remittances abroad from Australia require exchange control approval, in practice no restrictions are imposed on current (i.e. non-capital) transactions, and the Australian trading banks have been authorised to deal with the majority of these transactions as agents of exchange control on behalf of the Reserve Bank of Australia.

The Commonwealth Government has a taxation policy designed not only to encourage growth, but also to provide fair treatment for all concerned in the country's future development. Both the Commonwealth and the State Governments have power to make their own taxation laws, but in practice there is no general duplication of taxes. The main Commonwealth Government taxes are income tax, sales tax, customs and excise duties, all levied solely by that government. On the other hand, land tax,

Workman at Port Stanvac.

Acid plant at Wallaroo Fertilizers Pty Ltd.

stamp duties and payroll tax are levied only by State Governments.

Australia has concluded comprehensive agreements, to avoid double taxation, with Britain, the United States of America, Canada, New Zealand, Singapore and Japan. In addition, a limited agreement in relation to international air transport profits has been concluded with France. These agreements provide that income derived in one country is subject to tax in that country. The other country (usually the place of residence) also has the right to tax, but if it does so, it must allow a credit on the tax already paid in the former country. The Commonwealth Government recognises the contribution which overseas capital makes to the development of the economy and pursues a policy of welcoming overseas investment, particularly where it is of a kind likely to help in the development of the nation's abundant resources.

The Development and Investment Team

A group of high-calibre advisers has been selected by the government to form the State's Development and Investment Team. Its membership comprises senior administrators and experienced businessmen with sound industry experience and connections, who will ensure that expert advice and service is provided to all investors interested in South Australia.

The Premier and Minister of State Development, the Hon. David Tonkin, heads the team. He is supported at Ministerial level by all Cabinet Members and especially by the Deputy Premier and Minister for Mines, the Hon. Roger Goldsworthy, and the Minister for Industrial Affairs, the Hon. Dean Brown.

Mr. Matt Tiddy, as Director of State Development, reports directly to the Premier. Mr. Tiddy was recruited from a senior executive position with a major South Australian manufacturer. As chief executive of the team, he co-ordinates all matters relating to State development, and ensures that the best possible service is offered to businessmen in their dealings with government.

He is a member of the State Development Council, a body of experienced executives from the private sector, which combines its abilities to advise the government in policy-making as it affects industry and commerce.

Mr. Tiddy is supported by various specialist Public Service Departments involved in development—such as the Departments of Trade and Industry, Mines and Energy, Marine and Harbors, Woods and Forests, Tourism and Agriculture.

Mr. Bruce Webb, head of the Department of Mines and Energy, is closely involved with the State's extensive mineral exploration programme, the commercial exploitation of its mineral resources, and the proper development and use of energy resources. Recent discoveries of vast mineral deposits in South Australia, including gas,

oil, uranium, coal and copper, place Mr. Webb and the department at the centre of developments based on these resources, as previously described.

Mr. Lincoln Rowe, the Director-General of the Department of Trade and Industry, has come to the government from a long and distinguished career in the private sector. His role is to negotiate with investors to secure new industrial developments for South Australia, and to campaign to identify and attract appropriate new industries.

The Department of Trade and Industry is the chief agent for administering attractive incentive and assistance programmes devised by the government to encourage industrial and regional development.

The Small Business Advisory Council is a body supported by the Department of Trade and Industry. This Council supports the Small Business Advisory Bureau, which provides counselling, advice and problem-solving services to the small businessman.

For expert assistance in such matters as industrial land, factories, shipping, finance and infrastructure, the team has access to the overall resources of government departments and instrumentalities. These include the Department of Marine and Harbors, the South Australian Housing Trust, and the Department of Lands. Further support is provided by government representatives in Singapore, Tokyo, Hong Kong and Manila.

Mr. John Rundle, Agent-General for South Australia in Britain, is responsible for servicing and co-ordinating development, investment and trade matters in Europe. Mr. Rundle is supported by a small staff of trade and industry specialists, and operates in close liaison with the Director of State Development and the Department of Trade and Industry in Adelaide.

In South-East Asia the government employs representatives to assist with its

development and investment programme. These include Mr. Toyohiro Tanaka, Elders Japan Pty. Ltd., Tokyo; Mr. Tay Joo Soon, Asiaco Pty. Ltd., Singapore; Mr. Ian Davies, Elders Hong Kong, Hong Kong; and Mr. George Marcello in the Philippines.

The head of the Department of Agriculture, Dr. Jim McColl, is the team's source of specialist advice on primary production. South Australia is proud of its achievements in primary production, and expects future development of export markets for agricultural products and farming technology.

The Department of Tourism, headed by Mr Graham Inns, brings to the team extensive experience and expertise. As the tourism potential of South Australia is realised, the role of this department will expand rapidly. The Department of Environment and Planning plays an integral part in the development of South Australia. Orderly planning for resource and industrial development is a priority. Environmental Impact Reports may be required for some projects but an important aim of the department is to see that environmental requirements do not cause developers delays in their plans, by providing full information and assistance in the early stages of a development.

The South Australian Development and Investment Team has a balance between membership from private industry and the public service, together with representatives of various educational institutions and professional associations located in South Australia.

Encouraged and supported by this State, the team is seen as innovating, facilitating, and as counselling. It acts as adviser and sounding board, playing an important role in State development.

It also leads in liaison between overseas interests, the State Government, and South Australian businessmen. Interested investors are invited to use the free and confidential services of the team.

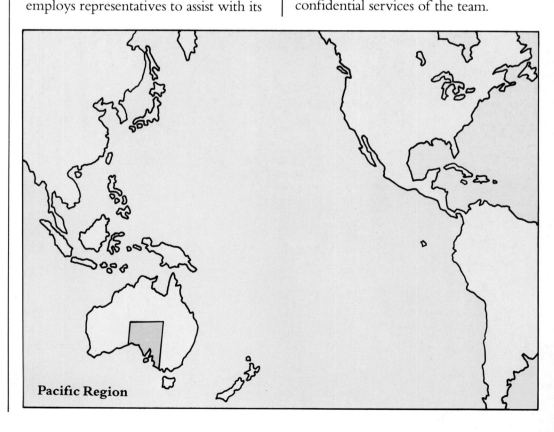

Pacific Region

Containers being offloaded at Port Adelaide.

COMMUNICATIONS: THE CENTRE OF IT ALL

South Australia is well served by all modes of transport, and communications networks link it with every part of the world.

A network of sea, rail, road and air services is well established between South Australia and the other Australian States. The central location of the State, and the Port of Adelaide in particular, means that South Australia is becoming increasingly important for importing and exporting.

Australian National, manager and operator of railways owned by the Commonwealth Government, is headquartered in Adelaide; the Port of Adelaide is equipped with roll-on/roll-off facilities; the Highways Department is maintaining and extending a network of sealed roads into other States; and Adelaide Airport is being extended to allow use by international air services.

Maritime

A vigorous policy of shipping development and marketing of port industrial estates is being pursued by the Department of Marine and Harbors.

Containerisation, specialised ship design, larger vessels and the impact of higher fuel costs have emphasised different handling techniques and fast vessel flexibility. A wide range of direct shipping services links South Australian exporters and importers with all major overseas trading regions. As well, large areas of industrial estates for port-related industry have been developed in the Port of Adelaide and major outports, and these are being intensively marketed.

The attraction of South Australia's Port of Adelaide and deep sea outports is their proximity to major population centres, mining and industrial developments to the north, west and east, and to markets. The South Australian port system thus has a hub position in the national handling and distribution industry.

Roll-on/roll-off berths, dredging, industrial land reclamation and modern facilities for commercial fishermen are the result of intensive trade studies in recent years by the department. At Port Lincoln, a 4000 tonnes per hour grain loader, positions South Australia at the forefront of Australian grain handling, while all deep sea ports have modern storage and shipping facilities capable of dealing efficiently with record harvests. As a consequence of regular dredging, the Port of Adelaide can now handle the largest ships using Australian ports. Proposals have been made to deepen the major ports and extension of the Port of Adelaide container and roll-on/roll-off terminal is projected.

"G" and "H" berths in the Port of Adelaide's Inner Harbor house Australia's only wharfside clinker plant, the cost-effectiveness of which has been demonstrated by market gains. The world's largest wharfside silo, to hold 30,000 tonnes of powdered cement, is also located on this site. In this way the department and private enterprise work in mutual interest.

Increasing Trade

Nearly one-third of South Australia's direct import trade is with Japan, and increasingly with South Korea. One-quarter is with North America and one-fifth with Europe and the USSR. One-eighth is with South-East Asia. More than one-third of the State's export trade is with the countries of the Middle East, while Asian markets account for about half of the total. The other main components are Europe and the USSR.

Sound management and control of import and export trade is crucial to the vitality of South Australia's economic resilience.

Frequent calls by a number of container shipping lines have already been established and the Australia-to-Europe Shipping Conference has initiated a fortnightly direct Port of Adelaide-U.K./Europe service. Other services have begun to the Middle East, South-East Asia and Mauritius.

The far-reaching economic disability of interstate trade diversion has led to the presentation of cases to other Conferences where direct shipping services with main overseas trading regions have not yet been restored. Negotiations will continue until a full direct trade flow is achieved. The department has had the full co-operation of the South Australian Chamber of Commerce and Industry, the S.A. Shipping User Group and a cross-section of maritime trade organisations in the preparation of its shipping representations. At executive level, discussions have been held in all of the relevant overseas trade regions, and these are continuing.

Other Activities

The department undertakes administration and policing of the Boating Act, under which pleasure craft are registered and their owners licensed. As well, the department provides moorings and facilities for marine recreational purposes, in conjunction with other government organisations and private enterprise. Commercial fishing vessels are surveyed, and operational facilities are provided in ports. A trawler-building and repair industry has been encouraged and provided with construction sites and slipways.

Control of navigation and implementation of internationally based legislation governing marine pollution, pilotage, engineering design, maintenance and construction of the ports system are all part of the department's responsibility. The duties of maintaining and administering river and lake ports increase with the growth in recreational boating and the inland water tourist trade. The department's Boating Branch polices use of the rivers and lakes for the Ports and Marine Operations Division, as well as patrols waterways to ensure safe use by pleasure craft, commercial vessels, water-skiers, anglers, fishermen and swimmers. Zoning of waterways for joint use is arranged in conjunction with local authorities and other government organisations.

The Department of Marine and Harbors' staff of about 850 persons includes a high proportion of professional officers and specialist tradesmen. It operates in a complex area of commercial and technical shipping and trade requirements in which the services and facilities provided play a key role in maintaining the State's competitive position.

Rail

Rail services in South Australia, except for Adelaide's suburban trains, are operated by Australian National (AN), a statutory authority of the Commonwealth Government.

The AN network comprises the former Commonwealth Railways, the non-metropolitan South Australian network and the former Tasmanian Government Railways.

From its Adelaide base, AN operates as a commercially oriented business enterprise, with efforts concentrated on bulk traffic, inter-capital freight and inter-major city freight. With nearly 12,000 employees, AN is one of the largest employers in South Australia.

AN operates a total of 13,235 items of rolling stock, including 324 locomotives, 11,028 goods and livestock wagons, 267 passenger coaches and 1326 service stock vehicles.

The combined railway carries approximately 12.7 million tonnes of freight and 510,000 passengers each year on a route length of 7687 kilometres. Comfortable overnight passenger trains with air-conditioned sleeping compartments are provided between Adelaide and other State capitals.

Railways in each of the other States are State-owned, but all railways are served by a joint marketing organisation called Railways of Australia, which ensures co-operation on matters of freight rates, interstate passenger fares and revenue sharing of interstate traffic. Therefore the customer has to deal with only one

railway—that of his State of origin.

The System

From Port Pirie, standard gauge (1435 mm) lines reach west to Kalgoorlie (connecting there with Westrail), north to Alice Springs in the Northern Territory and Maree, and east to Broken Hill, connecting with the New South Wales system. The lines between Broken Hill, Port Pirie and Kalgoorlie are part of the east-west transcontinental route from Sydney to Perth.

The Alice Springs line is part of the north-south transcontinental route being developed from Adelaide to Darwin. In November 1980 a new all-weather standard gauge railway from Tarcoola to Alice Springs was opened, replacing the narrow gauge.

The new Central Australia Railway is being extended from Alice Springs to Darwin completing a link first proposed over 100 years ago.

In 1983, conversion of the Port Pirie to Adelaide line to standard gauge will be completed, linking Adelaide with the interstate standard gauge network for the first time. As part of the $80 million project, a standard gauge connection is planned for the Port of Adelaide container terminal, in addition to the existing broad gauge line. A new road/rail terminal is planned for Islington in Adelaide and a new standard gauge marshalling yard is under construction nearby at Dry Creek.

Freight Trains

AN owns and operates, in conjunction with other railway systems, a wide range of specialist freight rolling stock to carry a vast range of commodities. Included is grain from country silos to ports, mills and merchants, bulk cement, maritime containers for export, timber, limestone, motor vehicles and minerals.

Roads

Main roads are constructed and maintained by the Highways Department of the State Government. Local roads are the responsibility of district councils, supported by grants from the Highways Department to ensure adequate standards.

In a State network of high standard sealed roads, the Stuart Highway north to Alice Springs is the only remaining unsealed national route in South Australia. However, upgrading of the 930 kilometre highway is currently in progress and is expected to be completed in 1986 at a cost of about $100 million. When completed this will boost tourism in the State by providing an all-weather road to the famous "Red Centre".

The 920 kilometre Eyre Highway (within S.A.) is the only sealed east-west road link. Upgrading of the this road across the Nullarbor Plain was completed in 1976 and it is now a major tourist attraction. The Dukes Highway, one of the most important rural roads in the State and the principal link with Melbourne is currently being upgraded and is expected to be completed in 1984.

The South Eastern Freeway, which crosses the picturesque Adelaide Hills, is

one of the main road links to the eastern States and is part of National Highway 1. Speed limit is an uninterrupted 110 kilometres per hour.

Regular ferry services are provided at 13 locations across the South Australian section of the River Murray, although, motorists may use five bridges at convenient locations.

Goods transport is free of control in South Australia and competition between trucking firms is keen. Interstate consignments are also free of control, under Section 92 of the Australian Constitution.

Motor coach services reach provincial and interstate centres on schedules conveniently arranged for business day-trips, or travel requirements between States. Parcel freight services are also offered by motor coach transport firms.

In metropolitan Adelaide, the State Transport Authority operates bus services with 800 buses, as well as 26 tramcars for the one remaining tramline, from the City to the seaside resort of Glenelg. South Australian transport planners are pioneering new modes of urban transport. Construction has commenced on 12 kilometres of O'Bahn Guided Busway to service the north east suburbs. When completed it will be the first use of this advanced system outside Germany. The Busway will gain international attention and its scenic corridor should attract substantial tourist interest.

Car registration stands at one car per 2.34 persons.

Air Services

By the end of 1982, Adelaide Airport will have an international terminal which will be serviced by Qantas and other international airlines. Direct flights are initially planned to New Zealand and Singapore, linking with flights to Europe. Interstate services are provided by both of the major national operators, Ansett Airlines of Australia and Trans Australia Airlines. Most parts of Australia can be reached from Adelaide with no more than one change of aircraft.

Adelaide has connecting flights to all overseas routes into Australia.

Within South Australia most population centres are connected with Adelaide by services operated by Ansett Airlines of South Australia. The company flies Fokker Friendship 44 seat turbo-prop aircraft. Services are frequent and scheduled for the business and personal needs of clients with good one-day timetables.

Charter flights, operated by several South Australian companies, are available to any part of the State at any time.

Fast and efficient air freight services are operated in South Australia by several companies. Total freight loaded and unloaded in Adelaide in 1979/80 was 21,206 tonnes.

Kangaroo Island Ferry

A regular shipping service operates between Port Adelaide and Kangaroo Island at a frequency of three or four round trips per week in summer. This

The railway line to Alice Springs near
Port Augusta.

depends on loading, and reduces to two round trips in the quieter winter months. Once weekly the service extends to Port Lincoln on the tip of Eyre Peninsula. Crossing time to the Island is 6½ hours on the roll-on/roll-off vehicle ship, owned by the Highways Department but privately managed. Passengers are accommodated in a lounge with aircraft type seating. The vehicle deck holds passenger cars, trucks and trailers. Nearly all products consumed on the Island are shipped from the mainland in this way. Back loading consists mainly of livestock for the Adelaide meat market, as well as passenger cars in both directions. Oats and barley are shipped from Kangaroo Island to Port Lincoln, from where superphosphate is transported to the Island.

Communications

South Australians are served by sophisticated networks of communications and media. Responsibility for telecommunication services in Australia rests with the Telecommunications Commission (Telecom Australia). This offers telephone and telex services nationally and internationally, with Subscriber Trunk Dialling and International Subscriber Dialling.
Through Telecom Australia, business personnel have access to both low and high speed link-ups with national computer banks in the Datel service.
A picturegram service is available to send and receive photographs nationally and overseas. This service applies to documents, X-rays, and other matter capable of being photographed.
The State has visual satellite hook-ups with most developed nations around the world. The giant Overseas Telecommunications Earth Station is a vital part of the State's communications system. Situated at Ceduna on the isolated west coast, and facing west, the Station provides satellite links with Asia, Africa, Europe and Britain through the Indian Ocean INTELSAT communications satellite.
Telecom Australia, through its South Australian office, also provides industry with a range of advisory services relating to all aspects of telecommunications.

Media

Adelaide has two daily newspapers, "The Advertiser", a morning broadsheet which is published Monday to Saturday, and an afternoon tabloid, "The News", published Monday to Friday. Adelaide's weekend "Sunday Mail" is one of Australia's biggest mass circulation newspapers. Locally produced ethnic newspapers are available along with a large range of locally and nationally printed specialist newspapers and magazines. Major overseas newspapers are also available, often airmailed into Adelaide.
The city also has four television stations—three commercial channels and the Australian Broadcasting Commission's ABC 2.
A wide variety of television programmes

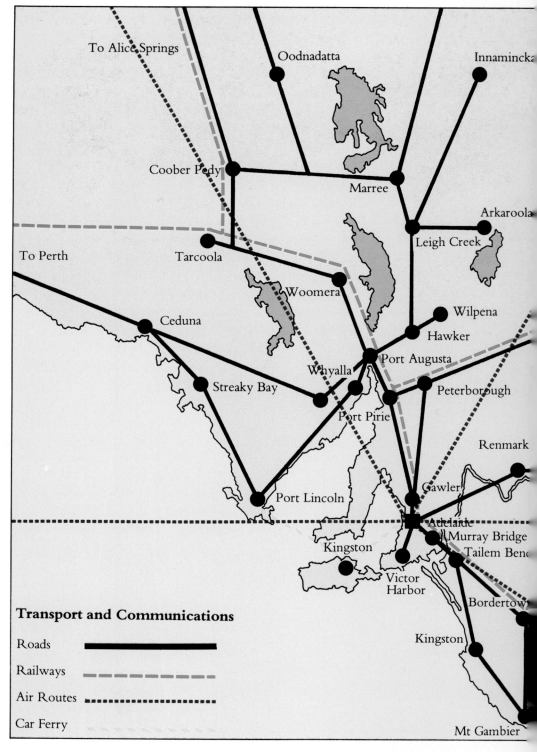

Transport and Communications

Roads
Railways
Air Routes
Car Ferry

are transmitted, some of American and British origin, and some produced in Australia. All stations must abide by a policy of broadcasting a certain percentage of locally-made programmes, many of which are of such a high standard they have been sold to overseas networks.

There are both AM and FM radio bands. On the AM band there are two ABC stations, four commercial stations and one public access station operated by the University of Adelaide. The FM band has one ABC station, one commercial and two for public access including an ethnic station which broadcasts daily.
Throughout country regions there are local newspapers, as well as radio stations and television channels or relay stations. A low-cost television receiving system has recently been introduced in Australia to give people in remote outback areas the opportunity to view television via the INTELSAT satellite.

Postal services are operated by the national statutory authority, Australia Post. Airmail and surface mail into and out of South Australia is co-ordinated at the General Post Office in Adelaide. Deliveries are made daily in all population centres in South Australia. Overnight Parcel Services and International Priority Paid Services are offered by Australia Post.

Video cameraman with news team.

Advertiser Editorial Room.

Freight handling at Adelaide Airport.

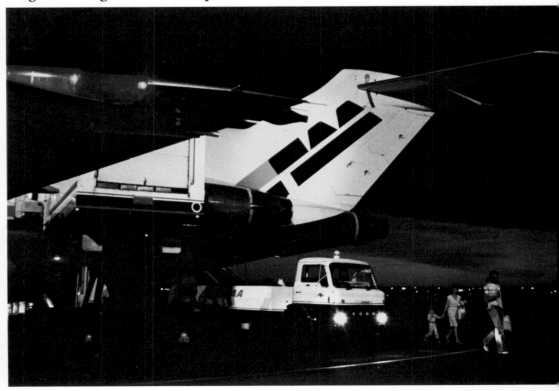

Mining operations at Iron Knob.

RESOURCES: UNDERGROUND TREASURE

Discoveries of vast reserves of oil, natural gas, coal, copper and uranium are generating a new era of prosperity in South Australia's mining industry. Record levels of exploration, both onshore and offshore, indicate the optimism of further extending already proven mineral reserves.

Two massive projects will lead the mining industry out of a period of decline into a period of exciting development.

The largest resource development project ever undertaken in South Australia is underway following ratification by the State Parliament of Indenture Agreement which provides for the recovery, processing and marketing of crude oil and condensate from the Cooper Basin in the far north of the State.

At Roxby Downs over $60 million is being spent in evaluating one of the world's great ore bodies containing copper, uranium, gold and rare earths. Assuming feasibility is proved, more than a billion dollars will be required to bring the deposit into operation later this decade.

Mining History

In its early period the colony of South Australia was able to grow from a struggling agricultural community to a viable, prosperous State with a sound, diversified economy. Copper mining effected this transformation and in the mid-nineteenth century 10 per cent of the world's supply came from South Australia.

The history of mining and the use of mineral resources in South Australia falls naturally into two major periods:

1840–1920 A period dominated by copper mining, an industry of world importance and a major employer of labour.

1920–1975 Iron ore from the Middleback Ranges led to the founding of the Australian iron and steel industry and the industrialisation dependent on these products. Industrial minerals were also developed during this period.

While many companies are now active in the field of metallic minerals exploration, local and export demand has caused production of non-metallic and industrial minerals and of gem-stones to expand.

Since the early 70s, energy minerals have become increasingly important and the search for them has intensified. New reserves of oil and gas are being discovered regularly in the Cooper Basin and there are encouraging signs in other areas.

Undeveloped coal deposits at Port Wakefield, Kingston in the South East, Anna-Sedan, Lake Phillipson and Wintinna are under intensive study. Samples of brown coal are being tested for combustion properties in application to power station developments.

Mineral resource development will continue to have a major influence on the prosperity, industrialisation and decentralisation of South Australia. In all areas the exploration industry is responding to the challenges of existing and projected demand, with high expectation of success.

There is a corporate confidence in South Australia's potential, which is receiving the full support of government. Enlightened mining and petroleum legislation is administered by a Department of Mines and Energy which provides comprehensive technical and information services and skilled contract and consultant services.

Energy—Now and for the Future

Exciting discoveries on the energy front give South Australians confidence for the future.

When the Cooper Basin liquids project comes on stream within the next two years, crude oil and condensate for Australian refineries will be available as well as LPG (propane-butane) for export and local use.

However, there is a pressing need to locate and evaluate all possible energy sources in a fundamental commitment of responsible government. Without energy, economic development cannot occur and lifestyles will be significantly depressed.

South Australia's energy use is in strong imbalance with known energy reserves. Coal, which provides only 26 per cent of energy use, accounts for about 90 per cent of our known energy reserves.

To correct this imbalance and maximise the use of indigenous resources and become independent of import fuel supplies, it will be increasingly necessary to locate and develop the State's coal resources. As well, there is a State-wide search both onshore and offshore by a large number of companies to extend the known reserves of oil and gas.

The Hydrocarbons

Commercial quantities of any form of hydrocarbons were not discovered in South Australia less than twenty years ago. The search began a decade before that when a company was founded by a group of South Australians who wanted to find oil. That company, SANTOS Ltd., now satisfies more than a third of Australia's natural gas requirements and is the operator for the billion dollar project to process and market liquid hydrocarbon.

The discovery of natural gas occurred almost by accident and it enabled the search for oil to continue. Other companies joined SANTOS in its search for oil and gas in the Cooper Basin and beyond.

Natural Gas

South Australia was one of the nation's first users of natural gas. Supplies first arrived in Adelaide from the Cooper Basin in November 1969. Construction of the 780 kilometres of underground pipeline was the consequence of agreement to use natural gas in the Torrens Island Power Station to generate much of Adelaide's electricity. Local, domestic, commercial and industrial use alone would not have been sufficient to justify the project.

The resources of the Cooper Basin are considered to be very significant with remaining reserves of 3.5 billion cubic feet. The Basin now provides natural gas for Sydney and Canberra as well as Adelaide so further exploration is necessary to meet requirements of the 21st century.

It has been estimated that about one-half of the ultimate gas reserves have been found to date. This has been achieved by the drilling of 100 exploration and appraisal wells. It is estimated that a further 150 wells will be needed to discover other reserves at a risk expenditure of at least $100 million. Successive State Governments have recognised the need for exploration and have progressively increased expenditure for an accelerated exploration programme being administered by the South Australian Oil and Gas Corporation.

The programme is being carried out by existing operators in areas away from the known gas producing areas as well as testing for extension of current fields. It is designed both to add to presently known reserves and to provide information on the ultimate reserves likely to be available.

Liquids

The importance of liquid fuels is particularly evident in South Australia where they account for 42 per cent of energy used. But energy reserves of crude oil are only 2 per cent of the State's total, so the local refinery at Port Stanvac, south of Adelaide, must depend upon imports of crude oil feedstock.

Development of petroleum liquids in the Cooper Basin will provide some crude oil feedstocks for Australian refineries and LPG for export and local use. These liquid hydrocarbons were found in commercial quantities in 1978—more than 20 years after the search began in that region.

The construction of LPG extraction and fractionation facilities at Stony Point near Whyalla, with a capacity to process 60,000 barrels per day, will unlock over 100 million barrels of crude oil and condensate representing about 5 per cent of Australia's current reserves.

As an indication of the magnitude of the Cooper Basin reserve, the 100 million barrels can be compared with the 15 million barrels of crude oil being run annually at Port Stanvac.

Oil flows recorded at Dullingari, Strezlecki and Merrimelia have assured commercial supplies will be fed into the Stony Point pipeline. Strezlecki No. 4 well tested 3600 barrels of oil per day which is the largest Australian onshore flow from a single reservoir recorded to date.

SANTOS, as operator on behalf of 10 other companies and biggest State holder in the Cooper Basin and liquids project developments, has scheduled the first processing of crude oil and condensates for early 1983 and beginning in early 1984, LPG will be available to the Japanese market. A contract has been signed with Idemitsu-Kosan of Japan for the supply of LPG for 5 years.

The Cooper Basin liquids development scheme involves the development not only of over 170 new gas wells on 23 new gas fields, for maintenance of contracted supplies of natural gas to the Adelaide and Sydney markets, but of the Tirrawarra, Fly Lake, Moorari, Dullingari and Strezlecki oil fields.

The production wells will be linked by 200 kilometres of gathering lines for initial treatment at a series of satellite processing stations on the fields. These in turn will be linked to the central processing plant by buried pipelines. After separation from sales gas the liquids will be piped to Stony Point, through 659 kilometres of pipeline.

Construction of the pipeline, facilities at Moomba and fractionation plant at Stony Point has begun, along with the construction of loading facilities and a 2.4 kilometre long wharf at Stony Point. The life of the scheme will exceed 20 years, during which time the bulk of the reserves from all currently known oil and gas fields will be produced.

Liquefied Petroleum Gas

LPG reserves in the Cooper Basin comprise about 7.4 million tonnes or about 90 million barrels. Estimated reserves are approximately three times this quantity.

A twenty-year development programme could involve annual production of 260,000 tonnes of LPG (3 million barrels or 500 million litres per year).

Apart from export markets, this LPG is becoming a substitute for petrol in South

Australia. Currently 1400 million litres of motor spirit are used each year in South Australia. Conversion of more vehicles to LPG will have a marked effect on the State's need to import crude oil for petrol.

Petrochemicals

Apart from crude oil, condensate and LPG, another hydrocarbon will be available as part of the liquids project. Ethane will be available in commercial quantities by 1984.

Ethane will provide a feedstock for a petrochemical plant should one be established at Stony Point, the Port of Adelaide, or elsewhere. An ethane-based petrochemical plant would provide further benefits to the economy of South Australia from the Cooper Basin resources. Such a complex would be designed to use ethane and locally produced salt to manufacture caustic soda and a range of petrochemical products. The rapidly expanding Australian alumina industry currently imports most of its caustic soda for the refining of bauxite to alumina and consequently there is a large and expanding market for caustic soda. Chlorine produced by electrolysis of brine for caustic soda is used in the manufacture of petrochemicals such as ethylene dichloride—the base building stock of the versatile plastic polyvinylchloride (PVC).

Coal

The earliest discoveries of lignite in South Australia were at Pidinga in 1885 and black coal was discovered at Leigh Creek in 1888. Other widespread occurrences of near-surface coal have been discovered since in basins of Permian, Triassic, Jurassic and Tertiary age.

Demonstrated and inferred reserves now total 9000 million tonnes, an amount well below the reserves in the Eastern States, but sufficient to guarantee South

Test drilling at Roxby Downs.

Coal mining at Leigh Creek.

The new experts—mining engineers at
Roxby Downs.

Australia's electricity requirement well into the next century. Such reserves of coal mean that South Australia, at this stage of its development, does not need to consider alternative power forms such as nuclear energy.

Coal has been a most important fuel in the development of South Australia and with estimated reserves being doubled in recent years it will remain a vital part of any future developments.

Leigh Creek

Since 1944, South Australian coal requirements for electricity generation have been derived from Leigh Creek. Almost two million tonnes of coal are mined annually by open cut methods. This is used at the Thomas Playford Power Station, Port Augusta, to generate about 23 per cent of the State's present electricity requirements.

By the year 2000 it is estimated coal-based electricity generation will satisfy 80 per cent of the State's total requirements. Annual consumption will be approximately 11 million tonnes of Leigh Creek coal, or its equivalent, which represents a cumulative requirement of about 120 million tonnes of Leigh Creek coal.

This requirement can be met at Leigh Creek alone. Recoverable reserves of over 130 million tonnes have been outlined in the Telford Basin at Leigh Creek. They extend to a depth of 200 metres and will be sufficient to supply the existing 330 MW Thomas Playford Power Station and the new Northern Power Station, also at Port Augusta, comprising two 250 MW units to be commissioned in 1983–84.

Expenditure commitments by the Electricity Trust of South Australia to supply the coal and additional generating capacity will include some $60 million for heavy mining equipment, $30 million for relocating the township of Leigh Creek to a site 13 kilometres to the south, and about $300 million for the new power station.

On present load forecasts, an additional generating plant will need to be operating by the late 1980s. Possible fuel sources for the new plant could come from a number of deposits which are currently being revalued.

Wakefield Coal Deposit

At the head of St. Vincent Gulf, extensive soft brown coals of comparable calorific value to Latrobe Valley coal are favourably located for consideration as the State's next coalfield development. Flat-lying or gently undulating seams up to 27 metres in aggregate with individual seams up to 15 metres thick occur at depths ranging from 60 to 70 metres. Recent drilling has shown reserves in the order of 2500 million tonnes.

A test pit has been excavated near Bowmans to recover a bulk sample of coal for evaluation in combustion studies. Assessment drilling, mining studies and geological evaluation are being continued.

Lock Coal Deposit

Several seams of high ash coal were discovered during the course of exploration by the Department of Mines in 1976 near Lock on Eyre Peninsula. Subsequent drilling has defined an elongated basin approximately 8 kilometres by 2 kilometres, with a number of gently dipping seams of coal having a cumulative thickness up to 18 metres, under cover of unconsolidated sandy overburden ranging from 40 to 100 metres thick. Indicated reserves are 150 million tonnes.

Lake Phillipson

Hard, black, steaming grade coals have been located 450 kilometres north-west of Port Augusta adjacent to the Tarcoola-Alice Springs railway. In 1905 a stratigraphic bore drilled to 988 metres at Lake Phillipson by the government intersected a number of seams of black bituminous coal ranging in thickness from 0.3 to 8.7 metres over the depth interval 50 to 143 metres.

Exploration undertaken since 1971 by Utah Development Company has delineated eleven seams greater than 1.5 metres in thickness, with several ranging up to 6 metres, under cover ranging from 50 to 100 metres. The deposits extend over an area of 60 kilometres long by up to 10 kilometres in width. Indicated and inferred reserves exceed 2000 million tonnes.

Kingston

The discovery of significant deposits of brown coal in the South East has been reported by Western Mining Corporation Ltd. Near Kingston, a seam 10 metres thick has been outlined under overburden ranging from 40 to 60 metres thick. Reserves are put at almost 1000 million tonnes.

Extensive drilling operations and the extraction of a bulk sample by large diameter coring have been completed. Samples are being tested to assess combustion characteristics and hydrogeological, geochemical and mining studies are in progress.

Anna–Sedan

The discovery of brown coal at Sedan by CSR Ltd. has significantly upgraded the Anna-Sedan deposits, 100 kilometres east of Adelaide. Drilling has been undertaken to outline about 300 million tonnes of brown coal in seams up to 10 metres thick at depths ranging from 35 to 60 metres. Samples have been recovered and studies are continuing.

Wintinna

Permian sub-bituminous coals were disclosed during stratigraphic drilling in the northern sector of the Arckaringa Basin by the Department of Mines and Energy. They are being explored by Meekatharra Minerals Ltd. and drilling undertaken has delineated eight seams of coal ranging from 1 to 7 metres in thickness under cover ranging from 140 to 280 metres.

Substantial tonnages of coal have been outlined and the deposits are currently

At work on a drill shaft—Roxby Downs.

being evaluated.

Cooper and Pedirka Basins

During the course of petroleum exploration, coal measures have been disclosed in these basins at depths ranging from 1400 to 4000 metres. Seams ranging up to 20 metres thick have been intersected. Resources, estimated at 3 trillion tonnes, dwarf all other proven deposits.

Mining of this huge energy resource would not seem feasible. In situ gasification following depletion of natural gas reserves, stands out as a possible technological challenge for the future.

Bituminous Shales

Dolomite, i.e. calcerous and argillaceous sediments intersected in the Byilkaoora stratigraphic well, drilled in the north-eastern part of the Officer Basin, is remarkable in that it contains oil seepages and organic-rich argillaceous carbonates with good petroleum source characteristics.

This discovery, while not adding to the energy resources of the State, has substantially upgraded this relatively little-explored region as a potential source of crude oil. Further, conceptual models establish the Officer Basin as being potentially favourable for the discovery of bituminous shales.

Summary

The proven energy resources in South Australia, the reality of commercial oil discoveries in the Mesozoic structures and the deep coal deposits of the Cooper and Pedirka Basins present challenging development prospects for future energy supplies.

Use of resources, particularly with regard to energy stocks, is of major importance to the economy of the State.

Non-energy Minerals

The non-energy minerals have been the

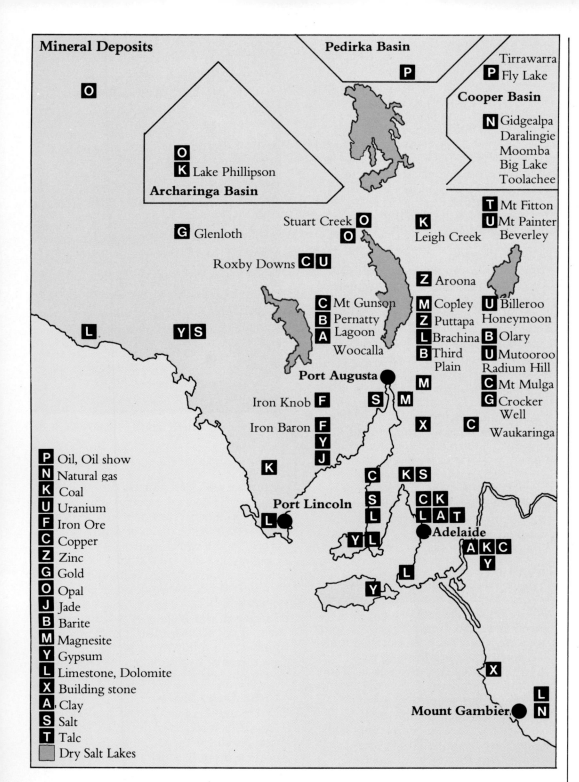

Mineral Deposits

Pedirka Basin

Tirrawarra
Fly Lake

Cooper Basin

Gidgealpa
Daralingie
Moomba
Big Lake
Toolachee

Lake Phillipson
Archaringa Basin

Glenloth

Mt Fitton
Mt Painter
Beverley

Stuart Creek
Leigh Creek

Roxby Downs

Aroona

Mt Gunson
Copley
Billeroo
Pernatty
Puttapa
Honeymoon
Lagoon
Brachina
Olary
Woocalla
Third
Mutooroo
Plain
Radium Hill
Mt Mulga
Crocker
Well
Waukaringa

Port Augusta

Iron Knob

Iron Baron

Port Lincoln

Adelaide

Mount Gambier

P	Oil, Oil show
N	Natural gas
K	Coal
U	Uranium
F	Iron Ore
C	Copper
Z	Zinc
G	Gold
O	Opal
J	Jade
B	Barite
M	Magnesite
Y	Gypsum
L	Limestone, Dolomite
X	Building stone
A	Clay
S	Salt
T	Talc
	Dry Salt Lakes

backbone of mining industry development in South Australia since the mid 1850s.

The importance of copper mining was replaced in the 1920s by the development of iron ore deposits. Now, 60 years later a new copper find, along with the discovery of uranium and gold in the same ore body, heralds a prosperous era ahead for non-energy minerals.

The Roxby Downs Project at the Olympic Dam site near the centre of South Australia is at the feasibility stage, with many millions of dollars being spent in the evaluation of deposits and the economic, social and environmental factors of such a major development. Further development of uranium deposits at Beverley and Honeymoon, at a cost of tens of millions of dollars, is imminent. Many companies are active in the field of metallic minerals exploration across the State.

In addition, the disclosed reserves of

high-grade iron ore will assure the stability of this industry for many years to come.

The Roxby Downs Project
The extent of mineralisation at Roxby Downs is of such proportion that it ranks among the world's single largest, new concentration of minerals to be discovered in 50 years.

Preliminary estimates indicate that the main ore body could contain 750 million tonnes of ore at grades of 1.5 per cent copper and 0.7 kg/tonne U_3O_8.

If the ore estimates are as indicated, Roxby Downs could contain more copper than the mines of Mount Isa and more uranium than the mines of the Alligator Rivers region of the Northern Territory. There is also gold present in the ore body as well as rare earth elements and other by-products.

At current prices the in-ground value of the commodities at Roxby Downs is worth in excess of $60,000 million.

Western Mining Corporation, an Australian company formed in 1933 to explore for ore deposits in Australia, discovered the ore body at Olympic Dam on the Roxby Downs Station in 1975. In the past, discoveries of copper and other minerals in South Australia were mainly as a result of prospectors finding surface outcrops. Today exploration is based on the sophisticated scientific approach. Geological concepts of ore formation and localisation are being allied to geophysical studies.

Western Mining Corporation took such a theoretical approach on the Stuart Shelf and achieved success after drilling only 10 holes at Roxby Downs.

The Roxby Downs deposit covers an area comparable with that of the City of Adelaide—6 km long by 1.5 km wide—with thick zones of mineralisation lying between depths of 300 and 1000 metres. Such a large tonnage of ore means that the operating company can plan for a large scale mining operation.

Western Mining Corporation and its venture partner BP Australia have proposed an eventual production rate of 150,000 tonnes p.a. of contained copper. This corresponds, at average drillhole intersection grade, to the mining of 10 million tonnes of ore per annum. In Australia this rate of mining is exceeded only in the mining of bulk commodities like coal, iron and bauxite.

It is anticipated that after mining, the ore will be milled to yield concentrates rich in the various metals. The products will support major secondary industries in smelting and refining, allowing for the export and fabrication of pure metals. An integrated approach to metal mining and processing will yield greater benefits to the joint venture, and to the nation, as income and employment, rather than will the simple export of raw mine products.

Uranium at Roxby Downs
The sales value of uranium at Roxby Downs would also be greatly enhanced if the product was refined and enriched. At this stage the contents of uranium remains to be determined, but it has been estimated that the deposit could contain as much as 500,000 tonnes of U_3O_8. If proven, this would make it the world's largest uranium deposit.

The uranium mineralisation is very fine grained and occurs in intimate association with the copper minerals chalcopyrite, bornite and chalcocite and digenite. Uranium minerals recognised include uraninite, coffinite and brannerite. The in-ground value of the uranium is in the region of $25,000 million.

The proposed scale of operations at Roxby Downs presents South Australia with great opportunities for decentralised secondary industry developments and associated long-term benefits.

With the processing of such large quantities of ore, extraction of even small proportions of subsidiary metals can contribute to income and provide the basis for significant related secondary developments. For example, recovery of a half a gram of gold per tonne of ore at

Roxby Downs could yield about 2 tonnes of gold annually, worth $25 million, and be sufficient to increase Australia's production by one-tenth. Significantly, rare earth and silver constituents of the ore could indicate secondary industry developments in product processing and utilisation.
If an integrated mining complex is developed at Roxby Downs, associated minerals can be utilised. Chief among these is hematite, which could be available for railing to Whyalla and blending with locally-mined ore.

Summary

The Roxby Downs project will benefit South Australia immensely. Preliminary estimates show that ultimately 10,000 and possibly 15,000 jobs could be created through direct employment on the Project together with indirect employment for the supply of materials and services.
The management of the project is required to operate within the legal and regulatory framework created by successive State and Federal Parliaments. A number of South Australian Government Departments will be closely involved in this process.
Like the Liquid Hydrocarbons Project, an Indenture Agreement will be needed between government and the project partners to clearly define the responsibilities and obligations of both parties.

Development of Mining

South Australia can boast not only Australia's first metallic mine (silver and lead), but also the nation's first gold mine, first copper mine and first smelter.
In 1838, two years after settlement of the colony, galena was discovered at Glen Osmond in the foothills of the Mount Lofty Ranges. This find, which was to be mined in 1841, marked the start of Australia's first mining era which lasted ten years.
By 1851, when gold was discovered near Bathurst in New South Wales, virtually all the metal mines in Australia were in South Australia. Some forty-nine mines were in existence. Thirty-eight of them for copper. These early mines included Kapunda, discovered in 1843, and Burra, the "Monster Mine", discovered in 1845.

Copper

Interest in the mineral potential of the newly established colony was stimulated and copper mining dominated the mining history of South Australia for the next 80 years. Between 1845 and 1851 the South Australian mining and smelting industry employed, directly or indirectly, most of the adult male population. From the first discovery of minerals until about 1851 the population of the State increased from less than 15,000 to 64,000. With some 900 copper mines in production at various times between 1840 and 1910, South Australia became one of the superior copper production centres of the world.
Over 300,000 tonnes of metallic copper were produced from the

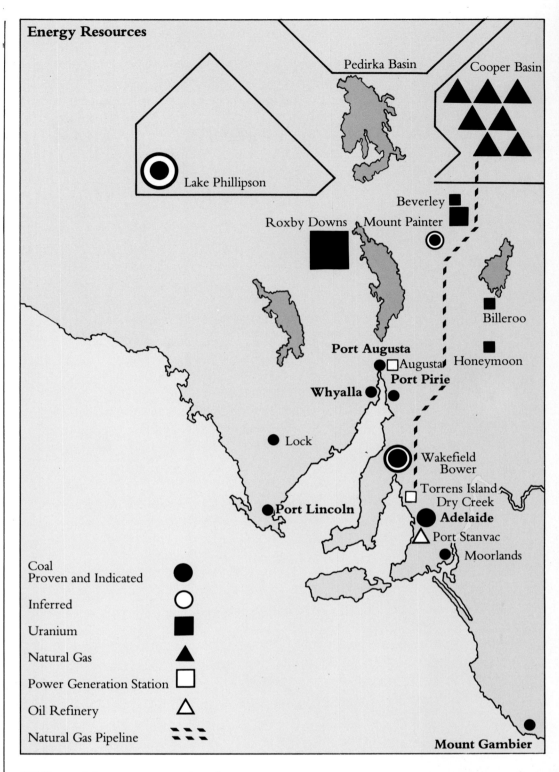

Energy Resources

Pedirka Basin

Cooper Basin

Lake Phillipson

Beverley

Roxby Downs · Mount Painter

Billeroo

Port Augusta · Augusta · Honeymoon

Whyalla · Port Pirie

Lock

Wakefield Bower

Torrens Island · Dry Creek

Port Lincoln · Adelaide

Port Stanvac

Moorlands

Coal Proven and Indicated	●
Inferred	○
Uranium	■
Natural Gas	▲
Power Generation Station	□
Oil Refinery	△
Natural Gas Pipeline	▰▰▰

Mount Gambier

Wallaroo-Moonta copper mines between 1859 and 1923, a production surpassed only by Mount Isa. Following the closure of the Wallaroo-Moonta mines in 1923, copper production declined rapidly with few discoveries being made since pastoralists and prospectors first covered the country locating and developing the easily recognised outcroppings of mineralisation.
Although the production of high-grade iron ore since 1915 has been important, agricultural and secondary industries have been the mainstays of the State's economy for the past 60 years.
Mineral exploration was revitalised in this State early in 1950, and increased with improved technology and back up services, financial incentives, the removal of export limitations in some cases, and most importantly, in response to a sequence of success in a variety of commodities in other States. This growth culminated in the exploration boom of 1967–1973.

Throughout this period, exploration of South Australia generally went unrewarded, with the exception of small-scale revivals of the old copper mining centres of Burra, Kanmantoo and Mount Gunson. The State's mineral industry declined again after the brief resurgence of the boom.
Recent events have altered this situation. It seems that by the end of this century, South Australia, while never again realising its former position of supplying a significant proportion of the world's copper consumption, could become the leading copper-producing State in Australia with an annual production of 150,000 tonnes of copper from Roxby Downs.

Iron Ore

From 1900, Iron Ore was mined in the Middleback Ranges, on upper Eyre Peninsula, for use as flux in the Port Pirie smelters, and from 1915 for iron and steel manufacture at Newcastle, N.S.W.

Moomba Gasfield installation

Petroleum Acts.

Publications and personal contact with experts within the Department expose corporate staff to a much wider view of exploration potential than may be available within their own organisations. By ensuring maximum availability of maps, reports and records of exploration, often in condensed or index form, the department contributes to the quality of information of the industry and the quality of exploration which can be performed by companies.

The department conducts exploration work in areas where more activity is thought to be warranted. The aim of such effort is to demonstrate a potential for economic mineralisation of a particular geological environment to encourage further private exploration interest.

Exploration in such cases is rarely advanced beyond an early drilling stage, at which point data is circulated and private companies are invited to apply for exploration licences. Thus the department acts as a resource centre for the promotion and stimulation of exploration activity.

Staff involved in regional mapping and correlative studies identify stratigraphic sequences drilled in exploration of poorly documented or concealed areas. This information and estimates of likely stratigraphy below, may facilitate a decision about continuation or abandonment of a hole.

The conduct of stratigraphic drilling to elucidate sequences in concealed areas is an important aspect of department operations assisting mineral and petroleum search.

Specialists in metallic, non-metallic and industrial minerals, regional geophysics, petroleum, coal, palaeontology, and hydrology are available for consultation. Other services offered by the department, not readily provided elsewhere, are in the field of biostratigraphy, fossil and micro-fossil identification, and aspects of seismic work.

Assistance in evaluating a prospect may be offered to prospectors or small companies with limited financial backing. The department may sponsor necessary research at the Australian Mineral Development Laboratories (AMDEL).

The work of most divisions in the department is concerned with the collection, organisation and recording of a geological information bank of the geology of South Australia.

Many of the drill cores resulting from private and departmental exploration, as well as other sample material, are stored in a highly accessible, indexed configuration in the new core library at Glenside. This has eventual storage capacity of $1\frac{1}{2}$ million metres of core, and ensures maximum benefit to the State from money spent on drilling by allowing continual re-examination of core after the original investigations are completed.

The Drilling Section, with a fleet of 32 rigs of various types, performs the services listed, including stratigraphic drilling for exploration and prospect evaluation, which directly benefit explorers. It also contracts work for exploration companies and other government bodies, but most of its work is to do with groundwater and petroleum investigation.

There is a well-established trend for exploration to advance from an area of outcrop, where mineralisation may be visually recognised or detected by geochemistry and geophysics, into areas where the host rocks are concealed below surface deposits. The latter type of exploration depends on "remote" testing techniques, such as geophysics and remote sensing imagery, coupled with advanced equipment technology and sophisticated interpretation. There is a reliance on drilling, as exemplified in the experience at Stuart Shelf, which led to the discoveries at Roxby Downs.

As the State's main resources and advice centre for the mining industry, the department is at the forefront of new developments. Continued research and drill-oriented field investigations are required to upgrade the quality of back-up information pertaining to concealed areas. It is part of the department's role to sponsor research which may improve exploration efficiency.

Likewise, the drilling staff are challenged to improve cost-efficiency by refinements in equipment, techniques and experimentation. Increasingly, with drilling often consuming 60-70 per cent of exploration budgets, efficient exploration will be dependent upon effective drilling.

Australian Mineral Development Laboratories (AMDEL)

Before its establishment as a statutory body in January, 1960, the nucleus of AMDEL was a research and development department within the Department of Mines, providing technology for the development of the uranium mine at Radium Hill and the uranium ore treatment plant at Port Pirie.

The expertise of the group was also used by mining companies to develop uranium deposits in Queensland and the Northern Territory. This generated further work of a contract research nature. During the 1970s this work has expanded to include work from the Pacific region.

Today, AMDEL is an independent contracting organisation providing technical, development and consulting services for industry and government in the mineral and material sciences.

Instituted by Act of the South Australian Parliament, the laboratories operate commercially and rely on earnings to provide the services offered.

AMDEL employs approximately 250 people in Adelaide at Frewville and Thebarton, with a further 50 being located at branch laboratories in Perth, Melbourne and Townsville.

AMDEL's extensive facilities are based mainly in Adelaide and provide services

Working in the smelters at Port Pirie.

in analytical chemistry, mineralogy, petrology, geochemistry, geochronology, materials technology, operations research, computer services, geostatics, mine planning, mineral engineering, chemical metallurgy, feasibility studies and plant design and commissioning.

AMDEL (Aspect) Pollution Consultants, has been established in order to co-ordinate and promote its efforts in the field of pollution and environmental control. It provides a comprehensive and integrated service for industry and government in investigations connected with pollution, environmental disturbance, control of the quality of the environment and in waste-management and efficient national utilisation of resources.

Clay scraping at Golden Grove.

RURAL INDUSTRIES:
WEALTH FROM THE LAND

South Australia is renowned for the quality of its wheat and barley, has produced Merino rams which have brought world record prices, and its forest management has become a model for enterprises in Australia and overseas. Half of the nation's vineyards are in South Australia, producing 70 per cent of Australia's wine.

The rural industries of South Australia, while restricted by the natural climate, make a significant contribution to the economy of the State.

The semi-arid Mediterranean-type climate of South Australia means that cereal production and livestock dominate the State's primary industry.

The rainfed farming system is a highly productive agricultural system which uses the limited resources of rainfall, suitable soils and manpower. Only 6 million of the 63 million hectares in rural establishments are devoted to cropping or permanent improve pasture.

The value of South Australia's agricultural production in 1980–81 amounted to $1341 million. Of this, $1005 million came from cereals and livestock, and the other $36 million from intensive animal production and horticulture.

Agriculture

The State can be divided into four main agricultural zones—pastoral, cereal/sheep, high rainfall and irrigated.

The pastoral zone comprises the vast area to the north and occupies 84 per cent of South Australia's total area. It is characterised by low and erratic rainfall of an average of less than 250 millimetres a year.

Livestock graze on natural vegetation such as native perennial shrubs and natural grasses in dry periods, while during and after extensive rain there is a proliferation of annual growth which provides good conditions for lambing and fattening cattle. The pastoral zone carries about 15 per cent of the State's sheep and 25 per cent of its beef cattle.

The cereal/sheep zone is the arable area of the State which receives rainfall of between 250 and 500 millimetres during the growing period through autumn, winter and spring.

South Australia is renowned for its integrated cereal/livestock farming system which involves the rotation of cereal crops with annual legume (medic or clover) based pastures. Legumes provide protein rich feed for livestock, increase soil resistance to erosion through increased organic matter levels, and their nitrogen fixing properties increase the nitrogen content of the soil for the following cereal crop.

The high rainfall zone is that area where falls exceed 500 millimetres. It occupies the southernmost parts of the State. The main bases for farming are sheep for wool and meat production, together with beef and dairy cattle. High value cash crops such as oilseeds, lupins, pasture and vegetable seeds and fruit and vegetable crops are also grown.

The irrigated zone comprises nearly 80,000 hectares of intensive crops such as vines, orchards, vegetables and pastures. About 23,000 hectares are fed from surface water resources such as the River Murray, while a further 55,000 hectares receive supplementary irrigation, mainly from groundwaters.

There is a considerable integration of cereal and livestock production within the zones. For example, breeding flocks are maintained in the lower rainfall areas of the State, producing sheep and cattle for fattening in a higher rainfall area. Some of the pasture seed required in the cereal/sheep zone is produced in the high rainfall zone.

A comprehensive description of the State's farming system is contained in "Farming Systems in South Australia" and is available from the South Australian Department of Agriculture.

Cereals

South Australia grows more than 12 per cent of Australia's wheat and about 35 per cent of its barley. Within the State's cereal/sheep zone over 2 million hectares of cereals are sown annually, producing an average of up to 4 million tonnes of grain. White grained spring wheats are the only varieties used but, because of mild winters, these are sown in autumn and grow through the winter months. South Australian wheat has excellent milling and baking qualities and is keenly sought by overseas buyers.

The State's barley crop is also sought on international markets because of its high malting characteristics. Large areas of land are cultivated, sown and harvested each year and this, together with the harsh climate and soil conditions, has resulted in a

unique range of agricultural equipment being developed in the State.

Companies like John Shearer Ltd. and Horwood Bagshaw Ltd. are exporting South Australian made equipment throughout the world.

Scarifiers and cultivators have been designed to cover large areas of land quickly and produce a desirable seedbed with maximum weed kill and moisture retention. Cultivation depth is shallow, by world standards, seldom exceeding 6-10 centimetres. The number of cultivations prior to seeding is tending to be less than the normal two or three times.

Seed is sown in autumn using a seed drill developed for local conditions.

The seeder places the grain beneath the fertiliser to allow maximum use of the nutrients by the growing crop. Grain is harvested in early and mid-summer and is handled in bulk from centrally-located silos. Wheat and barley are marketed through the Australian Wheat Board and the Australian Barley Board, both statutory authorities.

Oilseed and grain legume crops are becoming an attractive alternative to cereal grain production in some areas of the State.

Sheep

Sheep are produced in South Australia for both meat and wool. The State's flock is between 17 and 18 millions with about 3.5 millions a year being slaughtered locally and about 2 millions exported interstate and overseas.

The Strongwool Merino, which accounts for 84 per cent of the State's flock, was developed in South Australia to thrive under the harsh climatic conditions. The Bungaree strain, of which there are four parent flocks in the State, was developed mainly for the pastoral zone, while the Collinsville strain has the largest group of studs in Australia and its rams have brought world record prices at least four times.

Although it is kept mainly for wool, the South Australian Strongwool Merino is also a good mutton sheep. Merino wethers of between 50 and 60 kilograms liveweight are keenly sought by Middle East sheep buyers.

The average South Australian wool production is 6 kilograms of wool for each adult sheep a year, with sheep in the pastoral zone cutting 7 kilograms for ewes and 8 kilograms for wethers in most years. The average yield is 60 to 65 per cent clean wool.

South Australia has about 360 Merino stud flocks and in the cereal zone this variety is used for wool production while the ewes are joined with British breeds for meat production. Border Leicester rams are also joined mainly with cast-for-age Merino ewes to produce crossbred ewes. These ewes, which are the most fertile of Australian crosses, are mated with British breeds such as Polled Dorsets and Suffolks for meat production in the high rainfall zone.

Breeding stock of Corriedale, Polwarth, Cormo and Comeback types are available for export and are regarded as the best

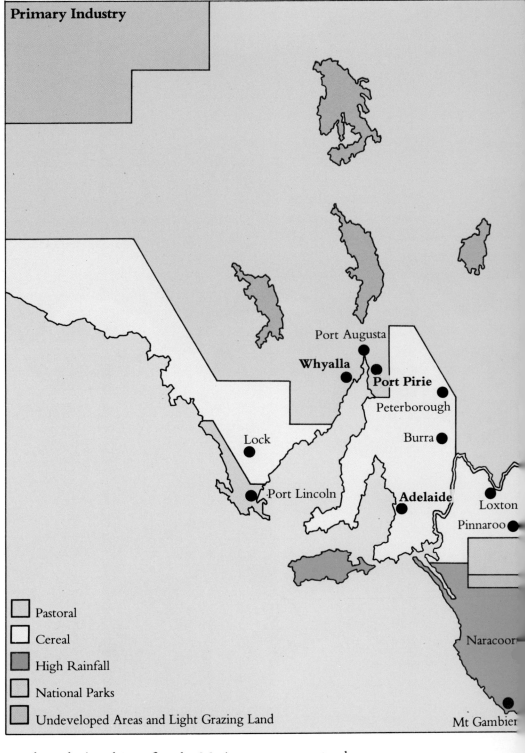

Primary Industry

- ☐ Pastoral
- ☐ Cereal
- ■ High Rainfall
- ☐ National Parks
- ☐ Undeveloped Areas and Light Grazing Land

wool-producing sheep after the Merino. The Border Leicester is particularly popular with overseas buyers.

Cattle

Beef production is South Australia's second largest livestock industry after sheep and wool production. In March 1981 the State's herd numbered 931,000, 60 per cent of which were in the high rainfall zone.

Most of the State's cattle are grazed on improved rainfed pastures while about 25 per cent are run under extensive conditions on unimproved pastures in the pastoral zone.

About 25 per cent of the State's beef production is exported with the balance being consumed on the local market. The preferred animal for the local market is 9 to 12 months old with a carcass weight of between 140 and 200 kilograms, while the main export demand is for animals of at least 250 kilograms, well-muscled but not fat. The United States is the main

export market.

The Poll Hereford, Poll Shorthorn, Angus and the Australian-bred Murray Grey are the most common breeds used to produce animals to service profitably the local market. Other breeds in the State include Hereford, Shorthorn, Red Poll, Simmental, Charolais and Santa Gertrudis.

Herd improvement is engendered by commercial competition. The scientifically designed and managed National Beef Recording Scheme encourages increased productivity of cattle, especially through objective measurement and recording of growth rate.

South Australia exports breeding cattle of the three main British breeds to many countries, although animals of other breeds are also available. Countries with mediterranean climates are likely to find breeds in South Australia which are ideal for their conditions.

The State's dairy herd of 160,000 head is

Tuna fishing at dusk in the Great Australian Bight.

mainly of Friesian and Jersey breeds. Herd recording and artificial breeding has created high production potential for milk and milk solids and the quality of the stock has resulted in increased export sales of heifers to many countries.
There is high local demand for milk and milk products as well as a developed cheese export market and this has allowed a reasonable return to producers. The average production of tested herds is 3600 litres of milk and 150 kilograms of fat per lactation, although some herds fed on grain concentrates average more 270 kilograms of milk fat.

Horticulture
Despite its dry climate South Australia has a vibrant horticultural industry which produces citrus, grapes, pome and stone fruits, nuts and vegetables. It is Australia's largest producer of citrus, almonds and apricots and the State's wines have an international reputation.
The Berri Fruit Juices Co-operative in the State's Riverland is the largest fruit juice processing factory in Australia. It handles an average of 50,000 tonnes of oranges each season and its sales total $36 million, forty per cent of South Australian oranges are sold to the fresh fruit market, of which 5 per cent are exported and a further 60 per cent processed into juice.
The South Australian wine industry dates back to 1847 when the first winery was established in the Barossa Valley. Today, half the nation's vineyards are in South Australia and produce 70 per cent of Australia's wine, 90 per cent of its brandy and 20 per cent of its dried fruit. The diversity of areas and grape varieties has resulted in an industry which has become world renowned.
More than 90 per cent of Australia's almond crop is grown in South Australia. This meets only 40 per cent of Australian demand so there is considerable scope for expansion, although high yields are necessary for plantings to be economically viable.
The Dried Fruits Board regulates marketing in South Australia of fruits such as dried apricots, peaches, pears and nectarines, and handles promotion of these fruits. Apples, pears and cherries are grown in the picturesque Adelaide Hills for local consumption as well as interstate and overseas export.
A small but active section of the horticultural industry is the production of flowers for export. Orchids cultivated in South Australia are eagerly sought by overseas buyers, while a new industry, the growing of native flowers for export, is emerging. Australian native cut flowers have a unique beauty which is being recognised in overseas markets.
There are a large number of market gardeners in South Australia, most of whom only cultivate a few hectares. The main market garden areas are adjacent to metropolitan Adelaide, in the South-East, on the coastal plain near Port Pirie and along the River Murray. The State is a potential supplier of table vegetables to the Pacific region, and the government,

together with commercial processors, is investigating trends in world vegetable demand.

Seed Production
A thriving seed industry in South Australia produces the basis of cereal and pasture crops not only within the State but also interstate and overseas. The Department of Agriculture issues certificates of guarantee for all seed grown and sold under the Certified Seed Scheme, ensuring both quality and purity. Certification is rigid, scientific and conforms to the highest international standards.
Researchers at Roseworthy Agricultural College, the Waite Agricultural Research Institute and the Department of Agriculture breed new cereal varieties for increased disease resistance and increased adaption to the local environment. The new varieties are multiplied by approved farmers in the Certified Seedgrowers' Scheme supervised by the Department of Agriculture.
New varieties of annual legumes, lucerne and perennial grasses are developed by plant breeders at the Department of Agriculture and Waite Institute. Additional information can be obtained from the Department's publication "Pasture Seeds from South Australia".
Formal courses in agriculture are offered at four levels in South Australia:
(1) Urrbrae Agricultural High School provides secondary schooling with an emphasis on practical agriculture in the field. This is suitable for farm workers and assistants to extension workers.
(2) The Department of Further Education provides post-secondary agricultural and horticultural courses and external studies programmes in agriculture.
(3) Roseworthy Agricultural College offers diploma courses at tertiary level in agriculture, oenology, natural resources and farm management. Diplomates are suitable for agricultural economic advisory work, however, their course has also kept them in touch with practical farming techniques.
(4) The Waite Agricultural Research Institute is part of the University of Adelaide and offers degrees and post-graduate courses in agricultural science. Graduates are suitable for advisory work and research.
All four institutions work with the Department of Agriculture, which also provides informal education through its district extension services.

Agriculture Department

Overseas Projects Division
An advisory service is provided by the Department of Agriculture to the State's primary producers. As a result of its involvement in research, advice and regulation the Department has established an Overseas Projects Division. This division co-ordinates the transfer of expertise that has produced a stable,

Harvest time.

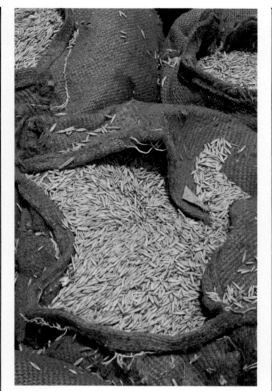

Bagged oats.

productive and profitable agriculture for South Australia. This technology has been utilised by countries with similar climatic and soil conditions, particularly in the Middle East. Expertise in fields like agricultural economics, ecology, form mechanisation, irrigation, pastoral management, seed certification, soil fertility/soil conservation and vine and tree fruit improvement has been shared with overseas countries.

Fisheries

Almost the whole of the South Australian coastline is fished commercially. The first Europeans to come to settle at Kangaroo Island were sealers and whalers, and today that region supports an industry of prawn, net and handline fisheries, as do the bays of the Coorong and the West Coast.

Tuna, lobster and shark are taken in open, offshore waters, and abalone on exposed coasts.

A new Fisheries Act introduced in March 1982, is administered by the Department of Fisheries and provides for licensing of fishermen and registration of gear. The department is particularly concerned with resource management, and control of fishing activity is maintained by licence limitations, the establishment of size limits, closed areas and closed seasons, the regulation of amount and type of gear, prohibition on the use of explosive or noxious substances in any waters and the establishment of aquatic resources.

Entry

While limited entry may appear to be against development, it is clear that more boats will not increase total yields from fishing operations. In this way South Australia has been recognised the world over as providing economic stability to its fishing fleets and the associated industries.

A provisional estimate of the annual gross value of the catch is $46 million.

Bagged barley.

1980–81 Fishing Production

Fishery	Lightweight catch (kg 000)	Value ($,000)
General marine species	5,456	8,218
Tuna	9,268	8,110
Abalone	938	3,285
Prawn	2,395	10,846
Rock Lobster	2,810	15,304
Freshwater Fish	720	401

In 1977–78, boats and equipment were valued at $54.6 million. Prawns, a most valuable catch, are a recent discovery. Western King Prawns were found in Gulf St. Vincent in 1968 and triggered rapid development.

In South Australia, fishermen participate in the formulation of policy and methods of managing the prawn fishery through the Australian Fishing Industry Council. Recently, this body has periodically closed some gulf waters, the biological effects of which are being investigated.

Rock lobster fishing is an old South Australian industry, which was boosted during the 1960s by the start of a lucrative trade to the United States. Lobsters are marketed by small groups of fishermen as well as large companies like SAFCOL. Processing plants are export-oriented, but there is a trend to promotion of local consumption.

SAFCOL Holdings Ltd. is the biggest fish purchasing, marketing and processing company in Australia. Headquartered in Adelaide, it has several plants in Australia and 10 in South-East Asia. Worldwide it employs about 5000 people and has an annual turnover of $135 million. About 50 per cent of its sales are outside South Australia.

Abalone is an important fishery requiring careful management, being susceptible to over-fishing, as growth to legal size takes 4 or 5 years and adults are easily harvested. Most of the catch is frozen and exported.

South Australia—German heritage in the
Australian environment.

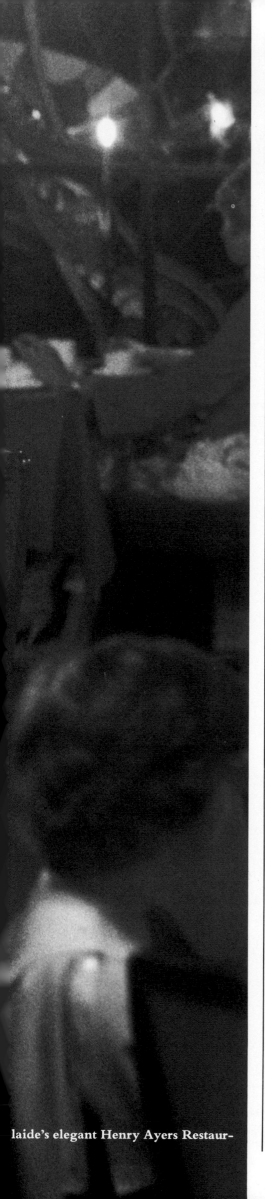
laide's elegant Henry Ayers Restaur-

TOURISM: THE PLEASURE IS YOURS

Natural beauty and friendly people are the ingredients for a successful tourist industry. South Australia has both, and much more.

The State offers the tourist a choice. International standard hotel accommodation is available in the centre of Adelaide, a city attuned to a variety of cultural activities. Alternatively, the tourist can spend a leisurely week aboard a small houseboat floating down the River Murray, accompanied only by the abundant birdlife along the river banks.

Whatever the desires of travellers may be, they need a tourist industry geared to meet their requirements. In the past decade, South Australians have recognised the importance of tourism as an industry. Millions of dollars have been invested in the provision of tourist facilities throughout South Australia.

The State has magnificent National Parks that are accessible to the public, many with camping reserves and amenities. Visitors can walk through areas of untouched country, and experience the sounds, colours and atmosphere of the bushland. Native birds, kangaroos, and native flowers abound. Within a few kilometres of Adelaide at the Cleland Conservation Park, small kangaroos and wallabies wander freely amongst visitors.

Apart from the beauty of South Australia's natural features such as the outback or sandy beaches, there are many tourist attractions built and operated to inform and entertain the tourist—such as the huge model of a rock lobster at Kingston in the South East, which stands 12 metres high to display the charms of the local fishing industry, or the cruise ship MV "Murray Explorer" which travels sections of the River Murray.

A Prosperous Industry

South Australia anticipates considerable tourist industry expansion in the 1980s. Tourism already provides a strong impetus to the State's economic growth prospects and the present rate of investment in the industry's future earning potential is extremely encouraging.

The development of tourism means promotion and expansion of local industries. Integration of tourism and industry is well-exemplified in the Barossa Valley. Its magnificent wines attract visitors to the cellar door, and these visitors in turn not only support the wine industry but also the regional economy through the use of tourist-service activities such as motels and restaurants.

An example of close integration can be seen in the Southern Vales wine producing region where two new wineries have been established with attached tourist facilities. The Old Clarendon Winery and Hazelmere Estates have been built to capture an old character and charm, yet offer the most up-to-date tourist accommodation facilities.

In other regions of the State, "man-made" tourist attractions have inaugurated an innovative period in the development of South Australian tourism. Though in their own right they are specifically commercial they relate forcefully to the region, and so benefit all local industry.

Increased momentum of growth in tourist investment can be expected as tourist-flows and patterns of expenditure are identified. The potential long-term value of tourism to commercial investors is evident on present trends and will become more so as development in South Australia is matched by promotion.

Conventions and Tourism

With the introduction of international flights into and out of Adelaide, overseas tourists can now fly direct to South Australia and stay in international standard hotel suites, like those provided by Adelaide's newest hotel, the Adelaide Hilton. The hotel, built at a cost of $40 million, offers 400 rooms of the highest quality. It will ensure that Adelaide has a favoured position in this crucial sector of the tourist market.

The opening of a number of new motels in Adelaide and country areas and the continued upgrading of other hotels means that South Australia's visitors have available accommodation of their choice.

Many hotels and motels are equipped to host small conferences, and coupled with Adelaide's venues for conventions, South Australia is establishing a reputation as an ideal place for conventions and congresses.

Adelaide can offer all the necessary infrastructural requirements for such events for small groups to those with in excess of 2000 delegates.

The "flagship" of the convention facilities in South Australia is the Adelaide Festival Centre. Superbly located within easy walking distance of major city hotels, the Centre has been host to numerous national and international

Suburban surf carnival at Adelaide.

Luncheon in the Southern Vales.

The Adelaide skyline.

Cockatoos at rest along Coopers Creek.

congresses covering a multitude of topics. Many tourist attractions are within easy reach from Adelaide's city centre—an important consideration in producing a balanced convention programme.

The important impact conventions make on tourism and the economy in general has long been recognised in South Australia and the Adelaide Convention Bureau strives to attract conventions to the State. Supported by State and local government, as well as the private sector, the Bureau offers a wide range of free services to the convention planner.

Adelaide—City and Surroundings

Adelaide began to create its own style of living during the sixties when a cultural revolution in planning, development, leisure and recreation occurred. A new sophisticated way of life evolved, enhanced by the pace at which business and leisure may be enjoyed in such a well-planned city.

Visitors to Adelaide remark upon the city's ability to have a "big country town" atmosphere, but not at the expense of the attractions and facilities of a modern metropolis. The city is served by more restaurants per head of population than any in Australia, with cuisine ranging from cheap meals over the counter in hotels to the exotic. Adelaide has an extensive range of ethnic restaurants including Italian, Greek, French, Lebanese, Chinese, Thai and Japanese. The city square of Adelaide, which is surrounded by a belt of parklands, is renowned for its charming old churches and hotels. At many street-corners there is either a church or hotel, built before the turn of the century out of local stone. The hotels, or "pubs" as they are often called, serve icy-cold beer to satisfy the thirst after a day in the sun.

Two restaurant developments in Adelaide within 15 kilometres of the city centre will become major tourist attractions.

On the coast at Glenelg a replica of the "HMS Buffalo", the ship that brought the first British settlers to South Australia in 1836, has been constructed. At a capital cost of $1 million it will serve as a floating restaurant and museum moored in a marina near the ship's anchorages in Holdfast Bay.

Another exciting development is a plan to site a large restaurant and other facilities at Windy Point, eight kilometres from the city and over 200 metres above the plain. Diners will have a superb panoramic view of Adelaide and its surrounding suburbs.

For devotees of colonial building styles, Edmund Wright House and Ayers House are typical South Australian examples. The latter, now the headquarters of the National Trust, was once the home of a State Premier. Part has been converted into a first class Edwardian restaurant, with a modern bistro also housed in the building, each with excellent table and cellar.

Adelaide, with its easy city access and excellent shopping in city and suburbs, is a pleasant and relaxing place to holiday. Within easy driving distance of the city are the Mount Lofty Ranges (or Adelaide Hills as they are commonly called) where one can see Italian market gardens, small villages of German settlers, farmlets, villas, art and craft galleries and studios, potteries, cheese and butter factories or vineyards and orchards, all of which offer hospitality to the traveller.

Further Afield

Because of its vast spaces, South Australia can offer tourists the experience of enormous contrasts.

A traveller can paddlewheel on the Murray or 4-wheel drive in stifling deserts; or perhaps ride in a 50 year old tram, or on camelback.

In country areas of the State the tourist-industry is witnessing a resurgence of interest and unprecedented

development. All regions have something different to offer.

The Outback

Australia's magnificent outback is unique. It cannot be described in words, it must be felt. People who have travelled to the inland areas of the Continent long enough to savour it, speak with awe of the sensation of silence, of space and timelessness, and of stunning colours and light.

Adelaide is the perfect departure point for the Flinders Ranges and beyond into the South Australian outback and the Northern Territory.

Sealed roads extend to the Flinders Ranges, then gravel roads take their place. Township pubs along northern routes offer adequate accommodation with standard hotel fare at low tariffs. In the opal mining towns of Andamooka and Coober Pedy, tourists can obtain a miner's licence and dig for precious opal. Four-wheel drive vehicles go on tourist safaris to many areas, including the Birdsville and Strezlecki Tracks, Cooper Creek, Lake Eyre and the Simpson Desert.

Flinders Ranges

One of the nation's most spectacular natural forms, the Flinders stretch from Melrose in the green pastures east of Port Pirie, to Arkaroola. In spring they are carpeted with exotic wildflowers. The Pichi Richi Railway, with restored steam engines, operates out of Quorn in school holidays and at other scheduled times.

River Murray

The houseboat fleet, with boats in a range of berth-sizes, is continually being expanded, and bookings are always heavy. The $2 million cruise ship MV "Murray Explorer" has joined her sister ship PS "Murray River Queen" to offer extended and day cruises. Both are outstandingly successful tourist ventures.

Touring by camel on Kangaroo Island.

Adelaide

■ The Outback □ Eyre Peninsula
□ Flinders Ranges □ Yorke Peninsula
□ Riverland □ Kangaroo Island
□ Lower Murray □ Mid North
□ South East □ Adelaide Hills
□ Barossa Valley □ Fleurieu Peninsula

Accommodation in river towns is excellent, and local attractions are linked with the produce and history of the region.

The Murray abounds in wonderful birdlife, and situated not far from the River is the conservation area for the hairy-nosed wombat, the State's fauna emblem.

Along sections of the river, archaeologists have discovered remains of aboriginal settlements so old, they have brought world-wide attention to their significance in man's evolution.

South East

The Blue Lake city of Mount Gambier is situated in an ancient volcanic region, which is now a centre for forestry, fishing and wineries. This is South Australia's most gracious provincial city, enjoying the benefits of its accessibility to and from the Western District of Victoria.

In Mount Gambier, a tourist attraction based on the local cheese industry is constructed of local pine and includes a theatrette, restaurant, souvenir sales area and factory observation area.

The Wine Regions

Synonymous with wine, the Barossa Valley is Australia's premier wine and brandy-producing district. A biennial Vintage Festival attracts many tourists to its wine, song, food and dancing, all in the traditions of its German settlers.

There are many pleasant picnic spots in the Barossa Valley, and local shops and restaurants complete the cultural feast with offerings of sauerbraten, garauchertes, apfel strudel and streuselkuchen.

South Australia, as producer of 70 per cent of Australia's wine, has other wine growing areas, all of which have developed their own particular characters and traditions, and offering attractive opportunities for tourists.

They include the Clare Valley, north of the Barossa Valley, the Riverland, Southern Vales, south of Adelaide, and the Coonawarra region in the South East of the State. Clare has its Easter Festival and in the Southern Vales a Wine Bushing Festival is held every year.

The Peninsulas

Eyre and Yorke Peninsulas are sea resorts, their main attractions being coastal fishing, sailing and swimming.

Yorke Peninsula is an area of ripening wheat and barley fields, fascinating to the student of colour and light.

In early settlement days, the townships of Moonta, Kadina and Wallaroo were important copper mining centres worked by Cornishmen. Each year the Kernewek Lowender (Cornish Festival) celebrates miners' culture with Cornish dancing and music, food such as huge pasties and the marvellous, mysterious drink called Swanky.

South Australia's capital was almost founded on the site of what is now Port Lincoln, Eyre Peninsula. The region has some of the State's best coastal scenery and offers excellent fishing.

The Tunarama Festival is held on the Australia Day weekend each January, to mark the opening of the tuna fishing season. There is dancing in the streets, a parade, aquatic events and a sail-past by the nation's largest tuna fleet.

Whaler's Way, near Port Lincoln, is a secluded coastal park with towering 120 metre cliffs, lonely surf beaches and deafening saltwater blowholes on the very tip of Eyre Peninsula.

Kangaroo Island is rich in fauna, and is protected from over-population by its large fauna reserve, Flinders Chase. Seals at Seal Bay cavort obligingly, for unobtrusive visitors, and mobs of kangaroo and wallaby graze in the National Park. The Island is easily accessible by air from Adelaide, or by sea on the MV "Troubridge".

South of Adelaide are the surf beaches, wineries and farming communities of Fleurieu Peninsula.

Victor Harbor has long been a popular summer resort of South Australians, along with nearby Goolwa at the Murray Mouth. Major tourist developments are currently being planned for this region.

The slate-roofed houses of Willunga with orchards and streams along the way, make this a pleasant area to visit, and a necessary port-of-call for those interested in Southern Vales' wine.

The Noarlunga Regional Centre is the natural gateway to the Fleurieu Peninsula. As a public-private enterprise joint venture this urban innovation offers a series of investment opportunities in an expanding centre of industry and population.

Whatever your specific interest may be, investment, industrial development, somewhere to visit for a unique tourist experience, or a new, clean, refreshing, uncomplicated, stable lifestyle in which to settle, South Australia has the answer. Come and see for yourself. You will be warmly welcomed by the government and the people of South Australia, who are proud of their heritage and proud of their State.

alking through a giant tube.

LIVING :
THE GOOD LIFE

Quality of life is a combination of economic well-being, cultural activity, climate, leisure opportunities and a stable system of government.

In South Australia the quality of life is excellent.

The standard of living is comparable to, or better than, that of the other States of Australia. The cost of a home is within the reach of most South Australians.

Apart from a developing, solid economy, South Australia has achieved an environment in which its people can enjoy and develop their own lives through an immense range of activities in their leisure time.

Flourishing creative activities are vital to the well-being of the community. There is a growing effort to widen the community's active participation in the arts.

In South Australia, it is recognised that cultural activities can be oriented towards the major population centre, Adelaide, to the detriment of other areas.

To benefit people in country areas, the Regional Cultural Centres Act was passed in 1976. Now the State is served by four Regional Cultural Centre Trusts, one each in the Eyre Peninsula, Northern, Riverland, and South-East regions.

Finance has been made available to improve facilities and for the construction of new buildings. The Arts Council of South Australia works to improve the frequency, range and calibre of work being done in artistic fields for country people.

All people of South Australia are benefiting from a Statewide effort to improve cultural opportunity.

The Arts

South Australia entered the twentieth century with its cultural base hinged on three main institutions, the Public Library, the Museum, and the National Gallery of South Australia. Each was housed in separate premises in North Terrace, Adelaide, which, having this spatial monopoly on the State's cultural venues, became established as its cultural hub, a position it maintained until the 1980s.

The Seventies, however, ushered in an unprecedented phase of development for the arts in South Australia, and since 1970 the range of available arts activities has been broadened and strengthened.

A large number of major arts organisations have been established here, or reorganised and, in many cases, standards have been raised to an international level. The amount of capital, both private and public, attracted to the arts, has increased significantly making it one of South Australia's growing industries and employers.

The Festival Centre, provides Adelaide with a major performing arts complex. The Centre, which cost $20 million when completed in 1974, is situated on the banks of the River Torrens adjacent to the city centre. It includes a multi-purpose concert hall and lyric theatre, two drama theatres and an open-air amphitheatre.

The Adelaide Festival Centre Trust, which administers the Centre, works either independently or with commercial entrepreneurs to bring to the Centre many Australian and overseas artists. The Trust commissions works of art for the Centre, operates the Playhouse Gallery and provides regular programmes of youth and community arts activities.

Festival of Arts

The Adelaide Festival Centre is the home of the Adelaide Festival of Arts Inc. As well as bringing notable overseas companies and artists to Australia, and providing opportunities for the first performance of major Australian productions and commissioned world premieres, the Festival includes programmes to attract greater community participation.

Every second year in March two to three weeks are devoted to this internationally acclaimed festival of visual and performing arts. Most of Adelaide's accommodation is booked out by festival-goers from South Australian country areas, interstate and overseas.

In the 1982 Festival some of the most popular attractions were drama and circus productions, ethnic dancers, buskers, clowns, and open-air cafes on the Festival Plaza, a craft fair in Elder Park, Flower Day and an opening fireworks display—by far the biggest display ever staged in Australia.

"Come-Out"

In non-Festival years a major arts festival for young people called "Come-Out" is organised by the Festival of Arts Inc. This began in 1975 following special grants from the State and Commonwealth Governments and a commercial sponsor,

63

The Savings Bank of South Australia. The festival of performances, workshops, exhibitions and other fun activities for young people is staged during the May school holidays, both in Adelaide and in country towns. "Come-Out" has become a model for youth festivals throughout Australia.

The State Theatre Company

The major theatrical company in South Australia is the State Theatre Company, formerly the South Australian Theatre Company which was established by Act of Parliament in 1972, as the State's major subsidised theatre company. By October 1974 the Company had moved into its permanent headquarters in the Playhouse in the Adelaide Festival Centre.

The Company is fully professional and presents a repertoire which includes classic and significant modern plays. The State Theatre Company incorporates the main "Lighthouse" acting ensemble and a youth activities group, the Magpie Theatre-in-Education Team.

State Opera

In 1976 the State Opera of South Australia was established by Act of Parliament as the State's subsidised opera company. As well as performing works from the standard repertoire appropriate for regional companies, the State Opera from time to time performs works of contemporary music theatre.

The Company stages regular productions throughout the year in Adelaide and South Australian country centres. School performances aimed at promoting interest in opera are a regular feature of the Company's activities. In 1979 State Opera purchased and remodelled the Opera Theatre to provide a base for its activities.

Australian Dance Theatre

During 1976 the Australian Dance Theatre was re-established and became the State's modern dance company. Its programme comprises seasonal adult performances, experimental or talent-finding workshop performances and a schools' programme. It is a measure of the Company's success that in May 1977 the Victorian Government also adopted the Australian Dance Theatre as Victoria's major dance company.

Carclew Youth Performing Arts Centre

The Carclew Youth Performing Arts Centre was opened in 1982 as the co-ordinating body and resource centre for the development of youth performing arts in the State. This unique centre, which occupies one of Adelaide's most historic homes, houses several national and international youth arts organisations and secretariats.

The Art Gallery of South Australia

The Art Gallery of South Australia, situated in the heart of Adelaide's cultural precinct on North Terrace, is one of the State's outstanding assets.

It's Centenary in 1981 won the Art Gallery widespread interest and support; important acquisitions included many generous gifts highlighting its extensive collections. Notable among them was a major work by the Australian impressionist, Charles Conder, "A Holiday in Mentone", and outstanding additions of silver to the decorative arts collection. The Gallery Foundation, formed to provide support for the purchase of high quality works of art, has raised $1.7 million.

The Gallery recently opened a newly designated display area, the Gallery of South Australian Art. This concept, unique in Australia, devotes a permanent space for changing exhibitions by South Australian artists from colonial times to the present.

Attendances have increased dramatically in recent years with exhibitions of international stature. During the Adelaide Festival up to 1000 visitors a day enjoyed the variety of works.

The Art Gallery's collections include Australian, European and American paintings, sculpture, a fine collection of 20,000 prints and drawings, furniture, tapestries, silver, glass and ceramics (which includes an important South-East Asian section).

Through the Travelling Art Exhibition and Outlook Programmes operated by the Education Section, the gallery tours original works from its collection throughout rural and metropolitan areas.

South Australian Museum

Boasting the finest collection of Australian Aboriginal Ethnography in the world, the Museum and adjacent historic areas are to be redeveloped and restored at an initial cost of $15 million. This redevelopment will be the first stage in an integrated development of the North Terrace cultural institutions, including the State Library, the Art Gallery, the History Trust and the Museum on the one site.

Constitutional Museum of South Australia

A unique institution on Adelaide's North Terrace is the Constitutional Museum of South Australia—Australia's only museum of political history. The museum breaks with tradition in that it is not a collection of permanent display artifacts. Rather, it stimulates awareness of the State's history through the nation's largest audio-visual history programme. Half the museum is devoted to its computer controlled programme "Bound for South Australia" which uses theatrical settings, *son et lumière* and multiple screen audio-visual effects to take visitors through the three main areas of the historic original Parliament House.

Now part of the History Trust of South Australia, established in 1981 to preserve and promote the State's history and incorporating the Birdwood Mill Motor Museum, the Constitutional Museum is believed to be one of the only two political history museums in the world utilising electronic communication systems—the other being the Reichstag Museum in West Berlin.

Arts Festival production of "The Makropulos Affair" by Leos Janacek.

Libraries

The State Library of South Australia has its origin in a collection of books assembled in London in 1834, two years before the province of South Australia was founded. In 1980 the State Library held 845,000 volumes. Several branches are incorporated in the State Library. They are Reference, Archives, Young People's Services, Country Lending Service and Adult Lending Services. In addition, local authorities operate a total of 74 public libraries and several country and suburban centres operate institute libraries.

The South Australian Film Corporation

Established in Parliament in 1972, the South Australian Film Corporation has been a significant catalyst in the redevelopment of the Australian film industry.

Some of its productions, which include "Sunday Too Far Away", "Picnic at Hanging Rock", "Storm Boy", "Breaker Morant" and "Gallipoli", have achieved considerable international success. It has just completed a major television series "Sarah Dane".

The Corporation also assists production by independent film makers by providing studio facilities and advice. It also has the sole right to produce or arrange for the production of films for, and on behalf of, the State Government.

Jam Factory Craft Centre

Originally known as the South Australian Craft Authority, the Jam Factory Workshops were established in October 1973 with the aim of developing a craft climate in South Australia through which the standards of workmanship and design could be improved to an international level.

tained glass at the "Jam Factory" Crafts
Workshop.

Skilled craftspeople are employed as workshop heads responsible for production and training programmes in crafts including glass, pottery and leather. The Jam Factory operates a prestigious craft gallery and a craft shop which markets not only items produced by employees but by independent craftspeople in South Australia as well.

Summary

Following rapid expansion, the arts in South Australia have become an important industry. More skilled and professional staff are required now in the arts than ever before.
In 1978, with assistance from the Government, a graduate diploma course, providing tuition in both the theory and practice of arts administration, was established in the School of Business Administration at the South Australian Institute of Technology. In 1982 South Australia hosted the first national conference of arts administrators during the 12th biennial Adelaide Festival.
During 1981–82, the South Australian Government, through the Department for the Arts, provided $12 million for the maintenance and development of the arts and cultural institutions. This includes grants to small arts organisations and individuals.

Education

Diversity is a common theme in South Australian education. Schools, colleges and universities are designed for students with widely differing needs.
Government and independent schools have been able to merge old and new into the contemporary system. Modern, open schools in pleasant surroundings teach with the most recent aids and techniques, but still emphasise fundamentals.
Curricula have been developed and adapted to cater not only for average students but also for the most talented and less able. There are no "special interest" schools which aim to provide for those with exceptional abilities in music and languages. A range of services supports those who have difficulty in coping with normal studies.
Agriculture is taught in the metropolitan area, at Urrbrae, and young people are prepared for work in the country regions of the State, for industrial as well as agricultural and academic opportunity.
Educators in South Australia are committed to a system which reflects the multi-cultural nature of their society, aiming to sensitise all the distinctive cultures that co-exist in Australia, attempting to foster, among children of immigrant parents, pride in their family's unique cultural and linguistic traditions.

Further Education

The Department of Further Education organises courses at 28 colleges throughout South Australia each year. More than 120,000 adults enrol annually. Courses are designed to enhance lifestyles, to enhance work and leisure opportunities, to develop talent, attain vocational skills, advance careers and progress towards the achievement of their aspirations.
Career studies offered include apprentice and post-apprentice education, Certificate courses giving recognised qualifications for industry and commerce, and short refresher courses to update skills and knowledge. All career courses are the result of close consultation with interested industries.
The department offers special education for special needs. This includes courses for unemployed youth, migrants, Aborigines, people with literacy problems, the handicapped, and transition courses for school-leavers.
Part of the philosophy of the department is that education is a lifelong process and that barriers to education should be removed where possible. Strict prerequisite qualifications are not insisted upon. Students unable to attend classes can study by correspondence with the Open College of Further Education.
Higher education is provided in five institutions throughout South Australia. Two universities, The University of Adelaide and Flinders University, are distinguished for their research programmes which are continued to the post-doctoral level.
The South Australian Institute of Technology and the Roseworthy Agricultural College offer courses which, like the Universities, have attracted overseas students. The South Australian College of Advanced Education has five campuses in the Adelaide metropolitan area.
All these institutions of higher education provide opportunities for study at both undergraduate and postgraduate levels, offering preparation for most professions. In 1980 there were approximately 29,500 students enrolled in higher education in South Australia.

Health

South Australia is a healthy state. This is due to the combination of one of the best hospital and health systems in Australia and an emphasis on making South Australia a healthy place to live. It provides an environment appealing to firms looking for attractive areas in which to base their operations.
The South Australian Health Commission was established on 1 July 1978 to rationalise and co-ordinate delivery of health services.
It is estimated that total public and private expenditure on health exceeds $600 million annually. This includes health insurance payments, expenditure on pharmaceutical and other products, payments to practitioners, and Commonwealth and State expenditure. The present value of capital held for health institutions is estimated to be well in excess of $1000 million.
There are five main categories of health services:
—Public health and public protection: legislation, statutory committees, licensing and registration come within this category, as do control of

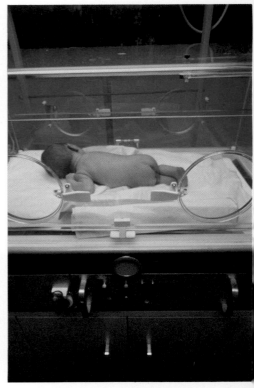

Neo natal clinic at Flinders University.

communicable diseases, and inspectorial and regulatory activities carried out by the central and local boards of health and the Environmental and Occupational Health Division of the South Australian Health Commission.
—Health promotion and maintenance: includes public education programmes on smoking, safety, drugs and other such issues designed to help people remain healthy.
—Primary care: is provided by health professionals in private and public settings. This involves about 1300 general medical practitioners, dentists, community health nurses, pharmacists and special organisations such as the Family Planning Association.
—Specialist medical services: are provided by specialist medical practitioners in both public and private settings.
—Hospitals: consume about 80 per cent of the State's expenditure on health. There are 123 hospitals, including psychiatric hospitals. Between them they offer more than 10,000 hospital beds.

Extended Care

For people with long-standing disabilities extended care services cover the following areas:
—Accommodation which is provided mainly by non-government organisations;
—Domiciliary care services offering a range of services to maintain people at home;
—Medical rehabilitation is an organised voluntary, community and institutional form of assistance for ill and disabled persons;
—Social rehabilitation is provided in day centres, senior citizens' and other group settings, on voluntary, community and organised bases. The South Australian Council of Social Services plays a major co-ordinating role.

Art class at Para Vista High School.

Flinders Medical Centre and University.

Mental Health Services
These are provided mainly by the Health Commission and by voluntary agencies. Two large psychiatric hospitals are included in the services. A range of specialist care assists patients to return to a productive life.

The Intellectually Retarded
The Health Commission and several voluntary agencies, most being State-assisted, provide services to care for the intellectually retarded. They include long and short-term residential care, day care hostels and sheltered workshops. Cramond House provides a Statewide diagnostic and assessment centre.

Community Health Projects/Centres
There is an extensive community health scheme in South Australia. Community health projects also include educational programmes for community health nurses, domiciliary care services, social worker support services for general practitioners, GROW groups, regional health services advisory committees, regional geriatric and rehabilitation services, community psychiatric services and the Foundation for Multi-Disciplinary Education in Community Health.

Dental Health
Comprehensive dental care is provided for disadvantaged people by the Dental Hospital in Adelaide, which brings together the Faculty of Dentistry of the University of Adelaide and the Dental Department of the Royal Adelaide Hospital. There is an extremely effective school dental service.

Aboriginal Health
Services include treatment, health protection and a health improvement service. The Aboriginal Health Unit provides these services to isolated communities. In settled country and metropolitan areas the Unit encourages Aboriginal people to use available health services, and concentrates on health improvement activities. The Unit trains Aboriginal Health Workers and liaises with Aboriginal Councils and community services. Funds are from the Commonwealth Government.

Family, Child and Adolescent Health
The aim of the South Australian Health Commission is to promote a coherent Child Health scheme from 0-18 years of age. To this end the Child and Adolescent Family Health Service has been established to co-ordinate services. South Australia has already achieved low rates of infant perinatal and neonatal mortality. The services also include institutional health care in most general hospitals and in the Childrens' Hospital as well as a range of community-based services.

Counselling and Welfare
Family planning, genetic counselling, marriage guidance, and family advisory clinics fall within these services, as do counselling for alcohol or drug abuse, or for victims of sexual assaults. These services are provided across the spectrum of channels of health care delivery from State to voluntary agencies.

Health Transport Services
While emergency transport is provided in remote areas by the Royal Flying Doctor Service, general ambulance organisation is carried out by the St. John Ambulance Brigade.
Some care and rehabilitation institutions operate their own transport services, for example this is done by the Regency Park Centre for Physically Handicapped Children and Bedford Industries Vocation of Rehabilitation Association. Local community buses often provide this type of service to residents, as do individual volunteers.

Aboriginal Affairs
In October 1979 the government formed the Ministry of Aboriginal Affairs.
The main responsibilities of the office are:
> To advise the Minister on policies and issues in the field of Aboriginal Affairs, including Land Rights and Mining on Aboriginal Land, to co-ordinate the special services provided by the State departments for Aboriginal people, and to liaise and co-operate with the Commonwealth Department of Aboriginal Affairs.

There is, as a result of the establishment of this office, an identifiable government aim to act at State level in the interest of Aboriginal people and to promote action on their behalf through other State departments.
The office is not a functional or service-delivery department, but rather an advisory one. Service-delivery rests with those departments whose responsibility it would normally be.
The Aboriginal Co-ordinating Committee reviews Commonwealth funds to special services provided by the State departments. Senior Officers of the Committee meet twice a year with Consolidative Committee members and the National Aboriginal Council to discuss financial and other matters.
Once a year the office is represented at the Australian Aboriginal Affairs Council where State Ministers meet the Commonwealth Minister to discuss Aboriginal policies and programmes.

Ethnic Affairs
With a total State population of some 1.2 millions, more than a quarter-of-a-million South Australians were born outside Australia. This creates a highly significant and multi-faceted cultural minority.
During 1980, the government recognised

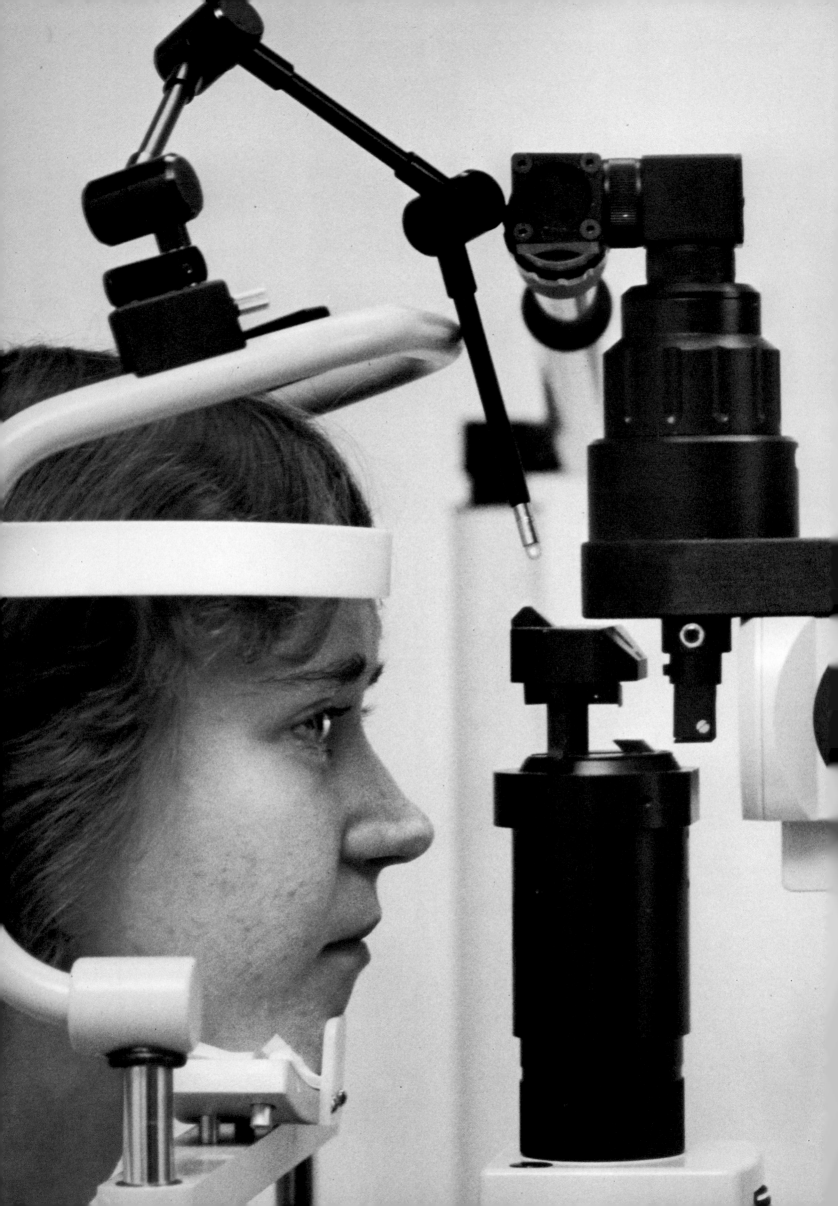

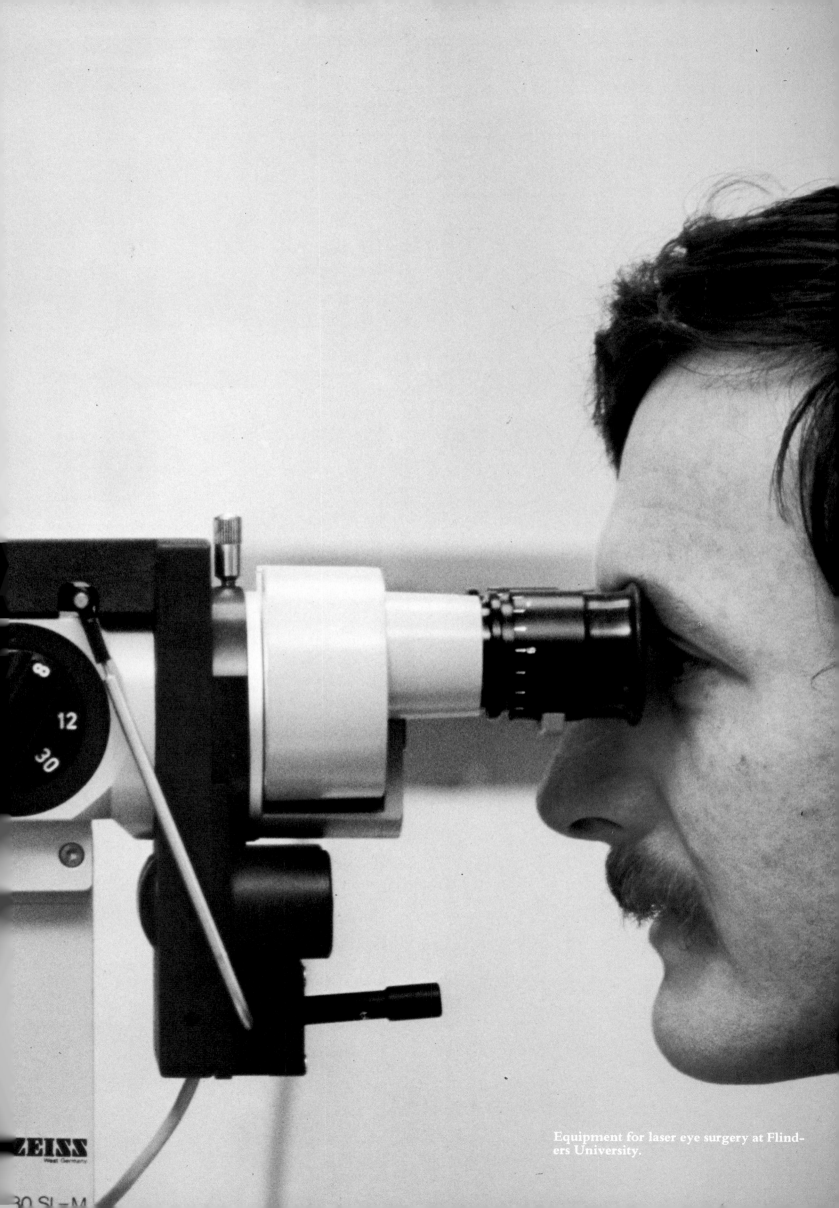

ZEISS
West Germany

8
12
30

30 SL–M

Equipment for laser eye surgery at Flinders University.

this significance by transforming the Ethnic Affairs Branch of the Department of Local Government to independent status in a separate Ethnic Affairs Commission, with a full-time Commissioner and seven part-time Commissioners.

The objectives of the Commission include encouraging full participation of all ethnic groups in the social, economic and cultural life of the community; promoting unity of all ethnic groups in the community while recognising their distinct cultural identities; promoting liaison and co-operation between bodies concerned in ethnic affairs; and advising the government and its agencies on matters relevant to and affecting ethnic communities.

The main functions of the Commission are to investigate, report and recommend on ethnic matters; to undertake research and data collection necessary for the preparation of advice; to advise on the appropriate use of funds for ethnic affairs; to consult with other agencies and organisations to determine needs and means of improving conditions affecting ethnic communities; to co-ordinate Government initiatives in ethnic affairs; to consult with ethnic communities; to promote greater awareness and understanding of ethnic affairs within the community.

Many of these functions already exist in the brief of the Ethnic Affairs Branch Project Section, which has dealt with such issues as: access to services; equality of opportunity; education; language and culture maintenance; ethnic arts and festivals; welfare; health and housing; legal and consumer affairs; labour and industrial relations; the aged; refugees; community relations and community development.

The branch has been the organiser of a State Interpreting/Translating Service which provides free interpreting services to courts in city and country centres. It also services State Departments, translating official documents, pamphlets, driving tests and such other matters as general correspondence.

A separate Health Care Interpreting/Translating Service is also available through health care institutions. The client contacts the relevant institution which in turn applies to Ethnic Affairs for the service.

The Ethnic Information Service provides reference and information services to non-English-speaking clients. The service is free and confidential, and conducted on a personal interview basis.

The community at large, however, may use this Information Service as a source of advice on migrant issues. The service is affiliated with a wider information network in the State, such as other migrant services, the South Australian Council for Social Services and the Citizens' Advice Bureau.

For its administration, the department is serviced by a series of committees which advise on funding for cultural events to special groups, conciliate and advise on discrimination, liaise with other government departments, and make policy on issues affecting migrants and police community relations.

Recreation and Sport

Most South Australians enjoy a lifestyle balanced between work and leisure. Growth in leisure time has meant corresponding growth in participation in recreation and sport.

The prevailing mild climate, extensive coastline of sandy beaches, accessible parks, gardens and wilderness areas provide ideal conditions for outdoor recreation activities.

High car ownership gives many South Australians the opportunity to drive for pleasure, caravan, and travel easily to beaches and parks. South Australians enjoy water sports such as swimming, surfing, boating and fishing.

Moreover, the wooded areas of the beautiful Adelaide Hills provide bush walks on trails and in scrubland, while the Parklands that frame the city square are natural recreation areas for family picnics, bicycling, and simply enjoying the gardens for people of all ages. Botanic Gardens, Conservation Parks and National Parks throughout the State are visited by many people.

There are opportunities to develop skills in over 70 different sports. The various sports associations offer extensive sports coaching in conjunction with the Division of Recreation and Sport. Much of this is in the metropolitan area of Adelaide but efforts are made to extend the range of opportunities to country people through regional and inter-club competition.

For its size, South Australia has achieved considerable national and international honour in such sports as football, cricket, tennis, athletics, squash, netball, hockey and basketball. It is a matter of some pride that smaller sports are not neglected, with increasing levels of participation in gymnastics, martial arts and many water sports.

The South Australian Government, through the Division of Recreation and Sport, has taken the initiative in upgrading and expanding a whole range of recreation and sporting facilities in city and country areas with the result that a network of multi-purpose recreation centres has been established throughout the State. These centres provide active and passive activities for both local residents and visitors.

Life Be In It

The State has supported a tradition of voluntary clubs and associations, and one of the strengths of leisure and sport pastimes is that people of all ages can be involved in almost any recreational activity of their choice, as participant or voluntary organiser.

South Australian sportsmen and women enjoy local government support for facilities and programmes serving people in their areas.

Private enterprise also plays a part in the provision of sporting and recreational facilities. Squash courts, roller and ice-skating rinks, heated indoor

swimming pools, golf courses, equestrian schools, health studios and amusement palaces are all initiated by private operators.

The "Life Be In It" campaign for national fitness and activity has stimulated recreational interest, particularly in areas like jogging, walking, swimming, bicycling and similar forms of regular exercise.

Special groups, such as the elderly or the handicapped, have received attention from project officers of the division, developing opportunities and, wherever possible, integrating these persons into existing organisations. Bushcraft and camping have been the subject of resurgence of interest in recent years. Voluntary organisations as well as the division can provide camping facilities for groups on educational, recreational or just social expeditions. Camps are situated pleasantly in the hills, or countryside or near the sea, sometimes in historic buildings. The groups which use such camps tend to be educational or training parties, business seminars or arts and crafts workshops.

International organisations such as Scouts and Guides have a loyal following in South Australia and provide recreational and educational activities for young people.

Fitness is fostered by the division through help to the Institute for Fitness, Women's Keep Fit Association, Research and Training, Health Centres, Y.W.C.A. and Y.M.C.A., recreation centres and other groups that may apply for assistance.

The division will continue to work with the community to provide a wider range of leisure opportunities for South Australians.

Housing and Construction

South Australians, and Australians in general, believe in home-ownership. Most can realise their goal and purchase a well-constructed house on a good sized allotment through bank, building society

Aboriginal child at an arts festival performance.

or other mortgage.

In the last Census (1976), statistics showed that 67.4 per cent of dwellings were either owned or being purchased. A feature of housing development in South Australia has been the change from the use of stone to brick as the major building material. In recent years brick veneer homes have become more popular.

The housing and construction industry in South Australia includes both private enterprise and the public sector.

A wide variety of housing types is offered by private companies and South Australia has major companies like A. W. Baulderstone Pty. Ltd. and Fricker Bros. Pty. Ltd. capable of major multi-storey developments and engineering projects.

A statutory authority, the South Australian Housing Trust, plays a significant part in the industry in South Australia.

Progressive development and the Housing Trust are synonymous. The Trust plans houses, shops, factories and community services throughout metropolitan Adelaide and in every sizeable community in the State. Its commercial and industrial projects support the development objectives of the government.

It is estimated that 580 hectares of suitable industrial land have been sold to other developers resulting in at least 550,000 square metres of industrial buildings. The Trust has also built and funded 57 factories and purchased a further 7 factories adding a further 330,000 square metres of buildings. It holds in excess of 500 hectares of suitably located industrial land in support of government-sponsored projects and to meet government development programmes. The Trust operates or has a continuing interest in 401 commercial units of various sizes.

These investments have been established to provide services and employment, to support government projects, to accumulate suitably-zoned land for such purposes, and to dispose of properties on advantageous terms or rates attractive to commercial investors.

The Trust offers substantial assistance in industrial development programmes by providing packages of houses, land and factory buildings, or any of these elements separately. Advantages offered under the government-sponsored, Trust-operated factory programme are well known throughout the State and the scheme is regarded as being a most important factor in the government's assistance to industry.

Throughout South Australia, housing is mainly 3-bedroom bungalow or villa detached dwellings. There are some high-rise flats and home units or town houses, but most South Australians live in well-constructed, light, airy, comparatively spacious houses.

Professional sub-divisional planning has devised building blocks large enough to ensure the privacy and spatial needs for individual households. Under the

Outdoor camping in the Flinders Ranges.

provisions of the Planning and Development Act, building blocks for detached houses in new subdivisions must be no less than 560 square metres, except in extraordinary, specially-approved circumstances.

Housing estates have been established primarily in relation to the State's industrial areas. These are well-defined and have been developed along main road and rail routes. The current building programme, public and private, metropolitan and country, continues on this basis. With housing so closely related to these centres of employment, commuter costs are minimised.

As the State's public housing authority, the Housing Trust has concentrated on building rental and sale houses in locations with easy access to industrial-zoned lands, giving priority to housing key personnel for industry. The satellite city of Elizabeth exemplifies the Trust's high standard of domestic and industrial development integration. Through State and Commonwealth Government funding, the Trust is the major builder of rental housing for low-income, handicapped, disadvantaged and aged persons.

For many years, because of the ample supply and relatively low cost of residential land, the emphasis was on large housing estates. More recently the tendency has been to build smaller groups of houses between the city and the periphery.

In the city and inner suburbs of Adelaide, local government and the Housing Trust have encouraged and accomplished restoration of existing houses in preference to redevelopment.

Community Welfare
South Australia's network of community services aims at helping citizens make best use of their community and human resources.

This web of services comprises voluntary, Church and government organisations. Within it, the Department for Community Welfare, with more than 45 district and branch offices throughout the State, provides assistance often in conjunction with the many voluntary and Church organisations in South Australia. Welfare services aim at practical applications and the provision of basic needs. Financial assistance is available; round-the-clock Crisis Care Service of the department provides immediate telephone counselling and on-the-spot assistance to people in the metropolitan area. Lifeline also provides a 24-hour counselling service. In addition there is also family maintenance and advice for deserted parents, foster care and specialised care for children whose parents are temporarily unable to care for them.

Other welfare facilities within the welfare system include women's shelters, youth programmes to develop work and social skills, budgeting advice and emergency accommodation.

Family First
A recent committee of enquiry

Vocational training at Para Vista High School.

established by the Minister of Community Welfare investigated the opinions of clients of welfare services. This unique study found that clients have become respected partners with the service providers, thus able to influence policy and organisational change.

Support of the family is at the heart of the Department's programme and philosophy. This is reflected in the enlightened Community Welfare Act, the Adoption of Children Act and the Children's Protection and Young Offenders' Act.

The department recently established a Family Research Unit to develop ways further to support and strengthen the family. It is developing a "family impact statement" for the use of government departments and agencies to measure the effect that decisions and legislation may have upon client families.

Inflation and increased social complexity present challenges to all welfare organisations. Continuing high unemployment, particularly among youth, is again causing hardship, stress and suffering in many families.

One programme, called Community Improvement Through Youth (C.I.T.Y.) has been successful in providing work experience for young unemployed and assisting community activities.

While many families and individuals come directly to the department for help, others are referred by a wide range of organisations, including health and welfare agencies, schools and child care centres.

In South Australia, volunteers, government and agency staff attempt to combat the problems through counselling, specially-designed programmes for youth, parents and the elderly, and wide-ranging projects for the treatment and rehabilitation of young offenders.

The recently enacted Children's Protection and Young Offenders' Act, is an innovative and advanced form of legislation which allows the assessment of offenders and provides for programmes to encourage them to become more responsible members of the community.

Specialised Supervision

Children's Courts can now order a young offender to follow a programme of training and rehabilitation, to do community work, to make restitution to a victim and pay compensation for damage, or be placed in secure care. Specialised supervision programmes are also available, and in recent years the number of young offenders have decreased.

Both screening Panels and Children's Aid Panels are unique to South Australia and have been successful in providing an alternative to sending all young offenders to court.

Children arrested or reported for offences are seen by a Screening Panel which decides if the child should go before an Aid Panel or a Court.

Children's Aid Panels may warn or counsel children or ask parents to provide

Haming it up at a suburban surf carnival.

a rehabilitative programme for the child. Parents must refer the matter to Court if the child does not admit the allegations, or if it is requested that the matter be dealt with by a Court.

Decentralisation of Community Welfare Department offices means that the services are more personal and close to homes of clients seeking support. This personal approach is consolidated by use of willing volunteers for community work. The department alone has 900 volunteers and hundreds more work for non-government organisations.

Each year about $750,000 is allocated to voluntary groups by the Minister of Community Welfare.

The ultimate aim of all South Australian welfare services is to provide necessary support to enable South Australians to develop real control and responsibility for their own lives, and to make better use of personal and community resources.

Police

The South Australian Police Force was established in 1838 and has played an integral part in the life and development of the State. It was first administered by a Commissioner of Police but has greatly expanded over the years and now needs a Deputy Commissioner and four Assistant Commissioners.

A precedent was set in 1915 when the South Australian Police Force became the first in the British Commonwealth to introduce women police officers. Since then the strength of both male and female officers has increased to more than 3000.

The maintenance of law and order is a priority within the South Australian Police Force. Its efficiency and high standards are reflected by the acceptance and esteem held of the police by the community.

The Force maintains criminal investigation branches throughout the State and these, together with auxiliary units such as Modus Operandi, Records, Fingerprints, Photographic, Ballistics and Laboratory, provide the skills and expertise necessary for the investigation of crime.

Great emphasis is placed by the Force on crime prevention. With co-operation from various security organisations, the police are creating an awareness of the need for social and business communities to accept responsibility for securing both personal and business property. An intensive programme of home and family security is being conducted by the Force and this has been enthusiastically accepted by the public.

The Force is continually trying to achieve the spirit of its motto "Salus Populi Suprema Lex"—the safety of the people is the highest law.

Consumer Affairs

Consumer protection is a responsibility shared by the State with the Commonwealth in its Trade Practices Commission.

The State Government's attitude towards consumer protection is that education is more important than legislation.

The Consumer Affairs Division of the department administers consumer protection, fair weights and measures and product safety and packaging.

The department also includes the Public Trust Office which handles about one third of all wills in South Australia. Staff have specialised skills in estate planning and administration. The office is 100 years old and has earned an excellent reputation in the community.

The Commercial Division includes the main licensing authorities for motor vehicle dealers, auctioneers, land agents, credit providers and commercial agents. It also handles landlord/tenant agreements and disputes.

The Licensed Premises Division deals with liquor licensing and places of public entertainment. The department also administers the Registry of Births, Deaths and Marriages in addition to the Equal Opportunity Division, which is responsible for matters under the Sex Discrimination Act.

Reflections in store windows along Rundle Mall.

Rundle Mall, Adelaide.

Golden moment on the River Murray.

YOUR SOUTH AUSTRALIAN
GOVERNMENT CONTACTS ARE:

Department of Agriculture
Grenfell Centre
25 Grenfell Street
Adelaide
(Box 1671 GPO, Adelaide 5001)
227 9911

Department for Community Welfare
G.R.E. Building
50 Grenfell Street
Adelaide
(Box 39, Rundle Street PO, Adelaide 5000)
217 0461

Department of the Corporate Affairs
Commission
8th floor, Grenfell Centre
25 Grenfell Street
Adelaide
(Box 1407 GPO, Adelaide 5001)
227 9911

Education Department
9th floor, Education Centre
31 Flinders Street
Adelaide
(Box 1152 GPO, Adelaide 5001)
227 9911

Department of Further Education
Education Centre
31 Flinders Street
Adelaide
(Box 2352 GPO, Adelaide 5001)
227 4204

Engineering and Water Supply
Department
6th floor, State Administration Centre
Victoria Square
Adelaide
(Box 1751 GPO, Adelaide 5001)
227 9911

Department of Environment and
Planning
55 Grenfell Street
Adelaide
(Box 667 GPO, Adelaide 5001)
216 7777

Department of Fisheries
16th floor, Grenfell Centre
25 Grenfell Street
Adelaide
(Box 1671 GPO, Adelaide 5001)
227 9911

South Australian Health Commission
Bank of NSW Building
52 Pirie Street
Adelaide
(Box 1313 GPO, Adelaide 5001)
228 0911

Highways Department
33 Warwick Street
Walkerville
(Box 19 PO, Walkerville 5081)
269 8911

Department of Industrial Affairs and
Employment
S.G.I.C. Building
Victoria Square
Adelaide
(Box 465 GPO, Adelaide 5001)
227 9911

Department of Lands
C.U. Building
44 Pirie Street, Adelaide
(Box 1047 GPO, Adelaide 5001)
227 9911

Department of Marine and Harbors
293 St Vincent Street
Port Adelaide
(Box 19 PO, Port Adelaide 5015)
47 0611

Department of Mines and Energy
191 Greenhill Road
Parkside
(Box 151 PO, Eastwood 5063)
272 5711

Department of the Premier and
Cabinet
11th floor, State Administration Centre
Victoria Square
Adelaide
(Box 2343 GPO, Adelaide 5001)
227 9911

Department of Public and
Consumer Affairs
23rd floor, Grenfell Centre
25 Grenfell Street
Adelaide
(Box 1268 GPO, Adelaide 5001)
228 3211

Department of Tourism
S.A. Government Travel Centre
18 King William Street
Adelaide
(Box 1972 GPO, Adelaide 5001)
51 3281
212 1644

Department of Trade and Industry
S.G.I.C. Building
Victoria Square
Adelaide
(Box 1264 GPO, Adelaide 5001)
227 9911

Woods and Forests Department
1st floor, Tinsmiths Building
135 Waymouth Street
Adelaide
(Box 1604 GPO, Adelaide 5001)
217 0402

OVERSEAS REPRESENTATIVES:

Mr J. L. Rundle
Agent General for South Australia
South Australia House
50 Strand
London, WC2N 5LW
England
(01) 930 7471

Mr Tay Joo Soon
Managing Director
Asiaco (Pte) Ltd
1202/1203, 12th floor
High Street Centre
North Bridge Road
Singapore 6
32 3077

Mr I. D. Davies
Elders Hong Kong Ltd
3716-3718 Connaught Centre
1 Connaught Place
Hong Kong
5-257395

Mr T. Tanaka
Elders Ltd
1001 Shuwa T.B.R. Building
7, Kojimachi 5-Chome
Chiyoda-ku
Tokyo 102. Japan
(03) 265 5291

Mr George T. Marcelo
1004 Wack Wack Condominium
Green Hills
Mada Luyong
Metro
Manila
Philippines
78 9906

SOUTH AUSTRALIAN
DEVELOPMENT CONTACTS:

Chamber of Commerce and Industry
(SA)
Incorporated
12 Pirie Street
Adelaide 5000
212 4691

Australian Mineral Development
Laboratories
Flemington Street
Frewville 5063
79 1662

Chamber of Mines
12 Pirie Street
Adelaide 5000
212 4691

The Government
of South Australia